JOSEPH FLETCHER: *Memoir of an Ex-Radical*

JOSEPH FLETCHER:

Memoir of an Ex-Radical

Reminiscence
and
Reappraisal

KENNETH VAUX, EDITOR

WESTMINSTER/JOHN KNOX PRESS   LOUISVILLE, KENTUCKY

Book design by Drew Stevens

Cover design by Kevin Darst, KDEE Inc.

First edition

Published by Westminster/John Knox Press
Louisville, Kentucky

This book is printed on acid-free paper that meets the American National Standards Institute Z39.48 standard. ∞

PRINTED IN THE UNITED STATES OF AMERICA
9 8 7 6 5 4 3 2 1

Library of Congress Cataloging-in-Publication Data

Fletcher, Joseph F.
    Joseph Fletcher : memoir of an ex-radical : reminiscence and reappraisal by the author of Situation ethics / Kenneth Vaux, editor. — 1st ed.
        p.   cm.
    Includes bibliographical references.
    ISBN 0-664-25372-5 (pbk. : alk. paper)
    1. Fletcher, Joseph F.   2. Ethics, Modern—20th century.
3. Bioethics.   I. Vaux, Kenneth L., 1939–   . II. Title.
BJ354.F541A3   1993
171'.7—dc20   93-4598

CONTENTS

Preface vii

PART ONE

1
The Complementarity of Humanism and Theism in Joseph Fletcher's Ethics
KENNETH VAUX

10
Casuistry, Situationism, and Laxism
ALBERT R. JONSEN

25
Fletcher the Matchmaker,
or, Pragmatism Meets Utilitarianism
MARY FAITH MARSHALL

PART TWO
55
Memoir of an Ex-Radical
JOSEPH FLETCHER

Bibliography: Works by Joseph Fletcher 93

PREFACE

MY THREE MENTORS in theological bioethics—Helmut
Thielicke, Paul Ramsey, and Joseph Fletcher—before their
deaths in 1983, 1988, and 1991 respectively, bestowed on me
the great but difficult honor of preparing for publication a biographical record together with reflections on their contributions
to the field of biomedical ethics. If only by reason of the sheer
volume and significance of their work, my stewardship has been
insufficient and tardy. I prepared for Thielicke a theological bi-
ography scheduled for the Word Press series Makers of the Modern Theological Mind, which has since been shelved. The Paul
Ramsey festschrift, containing one hundred pages of his own
final reflections on bioethics, is currently under consideration of
a publisher. The Fletcher conference, held in 1988 to assess the
career of the pioneer of situation ethics, produced a dozen essays, to which Fletcher added an autobiographical memoir.

While that larger festschrift still awaits a publisher, I offer
here Fletcher's "Memoir," prefaced by three interpretive essays—by myself, Al Jonsen, and Mary Faith Marshall. To these
essays I have added a comprehensive bibliography of Fletcher's
works.

In *Humanhood*, Fletcher offered a list of qualities that would constitute the presence of a person or a being with protectable humanhood. This series of attributes was found to be rooted in sentience, reason, and relationality. My essay notes the tension between the humanism and the theism of his early training in his provocative work.

Author with Stephen Toulmin of an important volume in recent ethics, Albert Jonsen contrasts the traditional casuistic modality of moral decision making with Fletcher's situationism. When we consider the wisdom of rabbinic case teaching or the refined nuances of Benthamite or Lutheran Pietist moralists in the nineteenth century, we see the perennial background of Fletcher's approach. In his essay, Jonsen affirms the validity, insight, and fundamental humanness of a case-focused ethic. And in an adaptation of her Ph.D. dissertation on Fletcher's ethics, nurse-ethicist Mary Faith Marshall shows the professional relevance of such person- and case-based work for clinical ethics.

Part Two, appearing in published form for the first time, is a delightful and candid memoir by Joe Fletcher himself. Extracted from a family diary that chronicles the colorful life of this kindly man, it ends the volume on a personal note. All of us who have been blessed by our acquaintance with Joe and Forrest Fletcher agree in the end that his impact on us stemmed from his warmth and support, his loyalty, and his steady inspiration. That he changed the course of American ethics and pioneered the field of bioethics is without dispute. His care for each of us and his love for the human family is even more certain.

Chicago
Summer 1992

PART ONE

The Complementarity of Humanism and Theism in Joseph Fletcher's Ethics

KENNETH VAUX

Frightened by the strangeness of their own arguments, most utilitarian philosophers fiddle with the felicific calculus so that it yields results closer to what we all think. . . . Without confidence in revelation we can only discover what we know. Philosophy is a second coming, which brings us not millennial understanding but the wisdom of the owl at dusk. There is, though, this alternative *revelation*, which I find more frightening than attractive: the wisdom of the eagle at daybreak.[1]

THERE ARE, of necessity, two great sources of the true, the beautiful, and the good—the natural and the supernatural. Mundane life reaches beyond itself for explanation. The eternal manifests its reality in the temporal. One source of the good is predictable, domesticated, and progressive; the other is uncanny. Intellectual, aesthetic, and ethical knowledge, like the rose, flourishes by virtue of both the soil and the sun. Earthly or natural reason is instinctive, obvious, and compelling, grounded in common experience. Reason of the heart and soul, transcendental or theological reason, is radical and visionary, often involuntary, strange, and disturbing. Since ethics requires both superficial and deep sensibility, both an autonomic and a mystic sense are required. The eagle flies by the clarity of dawn, but the brilliance may blind. The owl gropes in the dark but with accurate ultraviolet and infrared stealth. To fly, morality must have the nocturnal wisdom of the owl at night and the luminescent wisdom of the eagle at daybreak.

Our age has a fascination with ethics but a paucity of moral conviction and vision. Ethics has become an awkward fetish and a growth industry in this increasingly amoral age. The Harvard Business School has received a $25 million draft of guilt money from Wall Street for an ethics program but is not sure who should be the teachers. Should they use retread business school types or businesslike ethicists and philosophers to record analytic observations? Perhaps they should hire or co-opt humanists and theologians to present searching but alien visions. Again we ask Walzer's question about eagles and owls. As W. B. Yeats claimed, in our day the best lack all conviction and the worst are filled with passionate intensity.

Michael Walzer provides pioneering exodus through this wilderness. He contends that there are three paths of moral philosophy: the paths of *discovery*, *invention*, and *interpretation*.[2] The ethics of discovery are transcendental, tinged with *contemptus mundi*, ethics which in distrust of intrinsic norms draw norms from exterior patterns of good. Inventive ethics are pure artifact. Interpretive ethics, in some sense a synthesis of beyond and within, are what theology would call prophetic ethics. Prophetic insight sees into and through what is going on. This path of moral knowledge, in Walzer's phrase, "accords best with our everyday experience of morality."[3]

In this essay of tribute to the pathfinding work of Joe Fletcher, I will argue that he has successfully challenged the distance and danger of transcendental and theoretical ethics by reintroducing an ethics of the immediate and common life. In Michael Walzer's idiom, he has shown a moral path between "discovery" ethics and "despotic" or arbitrary ethics. In accenting the love imperative (agape), Fletcher has called on an interpretive insight that saves ethics from the treachery of unfounded absolutism and ungrounded subjectivism.

2

I will further argue that Fletcher's ethics are compelling where they are true to the prophetic nature of justice and agape. But rigor becomes rigor mortis in his system when these same ethics tend toward the principial and mathematical. I will develop this thesis by first sketching Walzer's notion of prophetic ethics and then scanning Fletcher's work for both its morally vital and its vitiated expressions. Summary analysis comes next. Finally comes my argument for the lasting value of bivalent ethics, with reference to the case of natality and mortality ethics.

In January of 1988, the Society for Christian Ethics honored Michael Walzer as one of the important moralists of our time. The society was long distinguished by the leadership of Fletcher and his sometime nemesis Paul Ramsey. Walzer's books *The Spheres of Justice* (1983), *Exodus and Revolution* (1985), and *Interpretation and Social Criticism* (1987) have taken their place among the salient texts of social and political thought. Coming on the scene with the kind of freshness that greeted Fletcher's *Situation Ethics* in 1966, Walzer's work creates a somewhat similar radical and provocative renaissance of moral discourse. It corroborates Fletcher's emphasis on a worldly and empirical ethic to counter absolutist and principial tendencies. It goes beyond to show the fallacy of an univocally situational or relativistic morality.

Walzer is skeptical of the two dominant types of modern ethics, the philosophy of invention and the philosophy of intuition. The one approach, reflected in Rousseau's social contract, in John Rawls's original position, or in Roderick Firth's ideal observer, contends that humans must create a minimal moral structure whenever they bind themselves in a community. Ethics are the primal construction of protection and affirmation in creating and maintaining cultural and political order. The second approach believes in some transcending or ideal moral reality, which is somehow then perceived and socially expressed. Between these paths of inventing a subjective ethic and discovering an objective ethic, Walzer argues that we might live best in moral freedom and excellence by seeking an interpretive ethic, one that searches out the *habitus*, or home of our actual moral living, and therein finds satisfying norms for life. Here the beyond is embodied in the within, the generic in the specific, the universal in the local, the eternal in the temporal. In the biblical spirit, I would call this an ethic of prophecy or exegesis.

Out of concrete historical process, a process of sifting and testing concrete moral prohibitions and possibilities emerges. David Hume showed, for example, how the ban on theft and the Lockean value of property had arisen gradually as a result of repeated experience of the pain of violation of that particular standard. Within the minimalist structures of such a "thou shalt not" morality, the rich textures of moral cultures are woven. These values and virtues take on authority as they become consensual and inspirational. They appeal to the common sense of good and they elevate the human spirit and provide an esprit de corps for the community. They evoke a sense of nobility, justice, and sacrifice, and they offer human satisfaction and fulfillment. In this sense they are prophetic and proleptic—they portray what we ought to be and could be. To depict this "common life" ethic, Walzer recalls the Deuteronomy text:

> For this commandment which I command thee this day, it is not hidden from thee, neither is it far off. It is not in heaven, that thou shouldest say, Who shall go up for us to heaven, and bring it unto us, that we may hear it, and do it? Neither is it beyond the sea, that thou shouldest say, Who shall go over the sea for us, and bring it unto us, that we may hear it, and do it? But the word is very nigh unto thee, in thy mouth, and in thy heart, that thou mayest do it.   Deuteronomy 30:11–14, KJV

Critical ethics is an ethics of argumentation and struggle, all expressive of an overriding truth to which all owe duty and obedience. Walzer retells this Talmudic and Midrashic truth.

Fletcher's ethic is also Midrashic, Talmudic, casuistic, and situational. The *Sitz im Leben*, the life context, gives shape to the good, not to predetermined principle or undetermined license. Fletcher would approve of the reassertion of casuistic reasoning as exemplified by the Jonsen piece in this collection and the following appeal by Walzer to the rabbinic tradition:

> The story involves a dispute among a group of sages; the subject does not matter. Rabbi Eliezer stood alone, a minority of one, having brought forward every imaginable argument and failed to convince his colleagues. Exasperated, he called for divine help: "If the law is as I say, let this carob tree prove it." Whereupon the carob tree was lifted a hundred cubits in the air—some say it was lifted four hundred cubits. Rabbi Joshua spoke for the majority: "No proof can be brought from a carob tree." Then Rabbi Eliezer said, "If the law is as I say, let this stream of water prove it." And the stream immediately began to flow backward. But Rabbi Joshua said, "No proof can be brought from a stream of water." Again Rabbi Eliezer said: "If the law is as I say, let the walls of this schoolhouse prove it." And the walls began to fall. But Rabbi Joshua rebuked the walls, saying that they had no business interfering in a dispute among scholars over the moral law; and they stopped falling and to this day still stand, though at a sharp angle. And then Rabbi Eliezer called on God himself: "If the law is as I say, let it be proved from heaven." Whereupon a voice cried out, "Why do you dispute with Rabbi Eliezer? In all matters the law is as he says." But Rabbi Joshua stood up and exclaimed, "It is not in heaven!"
>
> Morality, in other words, is something we have to argue about. The argument implies common possession, but common possession does not imply agreement.[4]

As with the rabbis, so for Joe Fletcher: ethics was a matter of argumentation, dialogue, and reason. I often remember him saying in those rare moments he resorted to theology, "The Divine Will must surely be like our sense of the loving thing to do." Rejecting the availability of transcendent and objective moral truth and the capacity for ethical certainty, Fletcher built a system of moral reflection on rigorous casuistic and particularistic foundations. Fletcher's career spanned the pilgrimage from theism to humanism, from revelation to philosophy. He was a laureate of the Academy of Humanism. The soaring eagle became the wise old owl.

Throughout his career Fletcher struggled against absolutist inclinations in ethics, especially when expressed in inhumane ideologies. These hardened and simplistic moral categories were often found in politics and religion. He was a pioneer of a more socialist and communalist ethics, in opposition to the excessive individualism and exploitation of capitalist economic ethics. When we read his autobiographical reflections in chapter 4, we see that he supported free expression over the anti-Communist McCarthyite suppression of free speech and assembly. Together with Gordon Allport of Harvard, Fletcher was among the first American professors subpoenaed before the McCarthy hearings. He advocated racial equality and opportunity in the era of sit-ins and bus boycotts. He constantly had to resist the calcified Christian social ethics of quietism and prejudice.

On the issues of women's rights, war and peace, environmental concerns, and the broad areas of sexuality, baby-making, health-care ethics, and concerns of dying, he similarly found himself in contention with those rigid ethical ideologies in church and society that ignore the particular personal and interpersonal pathos of the issues at hand. While Fletcher's reaction against these staid systems often gave a subjectivist and relativist tone to his own position, he did believe with conviction in moral truth and right beyond solipsism. His perspectives on two current and perennial topics—personhood and abortion, and dignity in dying—illustrate the exquisite blend of moral substance and situation that was the genius of his system.

Scarcely any current discussion on abortion can avoid direct or indirect reference to Fletcher's thought. As the Supreme Court in the 1990s qualifies and mutes the legal force of *Roe* v. *Wade* (1973), and as Justice Clarence Thomas helps adjudicate, the RU 486 question, we hear again allusions to Fletcher's ideas: "Is there 'personhood' in the fetus?" "Each 'situation' [case] must be judged on its own." The ideas about moral substance and procedure in Fletcher's ethics have permeated our culture's ethical reflection. Regrettably, the popular debate has not risen to Fletcher's case-by-case approach, nor has it accepted the helpful ethical tension he retained by balancing the deductive and inductive paths of moral reasoning: the flight of the eagle and the owl. Fletcher's thought on abortion illustrates this dialectic.

Fletcher devoted a large portion of his writings to the beginning of life. The general issues of human sexuality, genetics, prenatal diagnosis of abnormality in the fetus, and decisions regarding imperiled newborns occupied his thought for forty years. In his essays on humanhood he reflects on our "duty to the unborn."[5] He concludes that we have both individual and communal moral duties. Not only do we have a public health responsibility to provide vaccinations and inoculations against infections, we also have a duty to prevent the transmission of any communicable disease, even genetically rooted disorders.

Much of Fletcher's moral position on abortion is anchored on this altruistic impulse. He finds it unconscionable, in the words of a Catholic moralist, to "knowingly transmit" life in a diseased or debilitated state to another human being. He believes, with his lifelong friend Garrett Hardin, that community and ecological justice requires personal sacrifice. When challenged with the rectitude of an absolutist position that argues any life, no matter how grievously distorted, is better than non-life, Fletcher would appeal to the experienced moral sense of the mother and family as opposed to the abstract good of fetal sanctity or rights of the unborn. If this value of maternal and paternal experiential good prevails in abortion situations where there is fetal damage, it is also preeminent in abortions where there is no therapeutic import for mother or child. The mother's moral sense of what is possible, manageable, and bearable is the *ultimata ratio* of moral judgment. Well-being, accepting will, endurance, shalom—is the bottom line of ethics: "The ethical principle is that pregnancy when wanted is a healthy process, pregnancy when not wanted is a disease—in fact, a venereal disease."[6]

Fletcher's reflection on the personal and public tragedy of abortion helps us to see the heart of his ethical conviction.

7

Here is the utilitarian accent of his moral philosophy: What is the quotient between the good to be achieved and the harm to be avoided? He often speaks of his system as one of econometrics, of ethical mathematics. In contrast to the somewhat abstract and ideological slant of his later work, the springs and impulses of his ethics are more personalistic. As I have observed his teaching and clinical consultation, his writing and dialogue in hospitals, he is basically committed to the authority of a person over his or her own pleasure and pain, choices and sufferings, living and dying. "This is the person who must live with the decision," he would say. An unwanted pregnancy or unwanted terminal suffering under mechanical life support must never be imposed. It is not a doctrine of legal or philosophical autonomy that prompts this response, but respect and care for the plight of another human being. Personal experiences in his own life, including his wife's early work in birth control with Margaret Sanger and the death from cancer of his son Joe, a distinguished sinologist at Harvard, tempered this profound sense of identification and sympathy.

But Fletcher's ethics are not mere sentimentality. He is tough and uncompromising. Standing for and with persons whose life and well-being were on the line usually involved advocacy and fighting some adversary. Be it the racist sheriff in civil rights matters, the "pro-life" ideologue in an abortion case, or a technophile or legalist contesting the decision to withdraw a feeding line in terminal care, they had a real tussle on their hands with Joe.

Theism, or any heteronomy, was often the moral enemy to Fletcher. Importing any extraneous value that supplanted a person's sense of what was right and kind and possible was an evil force. Joe fought it with the tough rigor of his mind and the passion of his heart. Humanism was the focal philosophy in his ethics because it resisted the inhuman dictates of theism and kept attention focused on a person's plight rather than on abstract ethical principles. The one balancing ingredient to this emphasis in his ethics was his ecological and communal emphasis, which often led him to forfeit personal desires for the common good. While I don't recall his convictions on two

8

issues we faced in the 1960s in Texas—involuntary sterilization of Hispanic mothers after five or seven pregnancies and compulsory presentation of birth control knowledge and pills to black teenage mothers—I suspect sympathy with the community good of limiting further births might have found his support.

Similarly, he would support the rationing of exotic technological care for dying patients, to direct those resources toward more social goods. The heart of Fletcher's situation ethics is love effecting the common good or personal good, as that is compatible with the general good. What is that good in situations of birth, life, and death? Certainly survival is a primal good. Without life, no other temporal values are possible. But fragments of biological vitality devoid of consciousness and relationality and suffused with pain are not overriding goods. Values of quality in existence make it worthwhile. When we thus reflect on the heart of Fletcher's situation ethics, we come full circle to our initial observations about the empirical and down-to-earth manner of ethics and their complementarity with the ethics of transcending principle and power. The owl and the eagle fly in tandem. Practical problems in human affairs provoke decisions that point persons beyond their own resources. Transcending virtue, acts of love and hope, sacrifice and faith are manifest in the daily and mundane. This has been the genius of Fletcher's contribution.

Notes

1. Michael Walzer, *Interpretation and Social Criticism* (Cambridge, Mass.: Harvard University Press, 1987), 78, italics mine.
2. Ibid., 3.
3. Ibid.
4. Ibid., 31–32.
5. Joseph Fletcher, *Humanhood*, 138.
6. Ibid.

Casuistry, Situationism, and Laxism

ALBERT R. JONSEN

CASUISTRY IS an old word; situationism is a new one. "Casuistry" appears, according to the *Oxford English Dictionary* in Alexander Pope's *Rape of the Lock* (1725): "cages for gnats . . . and tomes of casuistry." The seeds of casuistry as a mode of moral discourse were sown by the Greek Sophists, nurtured by Aristotle's teaching on practical reasoning, cultivated by Cicero and the Stoics, disseminated widely in the canonical and confessional literature of the Middle Ages, and raised to maturity by the moral theologians of the Renaissance. Its respectability as a method of resolving "cases of conscience" was impugned in Blaise Pascal's *Provincial Letters* (1656), and the word has borne a pejorative connotation ever since.[1]

"Situationism" is of more recent coinage. It appears in the literature of and about existential philosophy in the late 1940s and gained prominence after a fulminating condemnation by Pope Pius XII in 1952.[2] Theologians both Catholic and Protestant discussed it extensively during the 1960s.[3] It can be said that Joseph Fletcher's book *Situation Ethics* made it a household word, or at least a pulpit and classroom one.[4] Despite Fletcher's enthusiastic advocacy, like many other "isms," it joined casuistry as a pejorative term.

Casuistry and situationism share a tarnished reputation because both are accused of fostering moral laxism. This was Pascal's principal charge: "Let them [the casuists] consider before God how . . . scandalous and excessive is the moral licence which they have introduced."[5] Criticism of Fletcher frequently asserted that "without genuine moral principles, a judgment of mere personal preference replaces a true moral judgment."[6] The Renaissance casuists could be charged with laxism because they excelled, as Pascal said, "in interpreting terms and observing favorable circumstances"[7] so that, regardless of how strong the moral law, they could find ways to interpret it out of existence in any particular set of circumstances. The modern situationists, eschewing the rigidity of legalism, emphasize the uniqueness of each situation in which moral decisions must be made and urge that decision be guided by "what love demands in the situation" rather than by remote and inflexible rules. It is easy to see how both approaches could lead to an ethics that answers every moral question with "Well, it all depends." This is, in the minds of some moralists, the very maxim of laxity.

Casuistry and situationism are, then, tarred with the same brush. But common adversity does not unite casuists and situationists, who seem anxious to avoid being seen in each other's company. From the earliest days of situationism, Catholic moral theologians recognized the similarities with their traditional casuistry and took great pains to distinguish between the reprehensible situationism and the reputable (although somewhat degenerate) casuistry.[8]

Fletcher himself is ambivalent. He is attracted to casuistry's willingness to "observe favorable circumstances" and to respect the uniqueness of situations. He approves of its being "case-focused and concrete, concerned to bring Christian imperatives into practical operation." He goes so far as to describe situationism as a "neocasuistry" and to speak of "love's casuistry" and a "casuistry obedient to love."[9] Despite this attraction, he is critical of casuistry because it is an ally of his worst enemy, legalism. The casuists, he believes, make rules about how to avoid rules. It is, in its twisting and bending of law, a plea for mercy that wins "at least partial release from law's cold abstractions. Casuistry is the homage paid by legalism to the love of persons, and to realism about life's relativities." Merciful and realistic though it is, classical casuistry is in bondage to legalism.[10]

Clearly, casuistry and situationism are related concepts, but the relationship is uneasy, uncertain, cautious, sometimes courteous and sometimes hostile. As I go about the task of rehabilitating the reputation of casuistry that Stephen Toulmin and I have inaugurated, I am frequently asked, "Well, what is the difference between your casuistry and Fletcher's situationism? How does casuistry avoid relativism?" The remainder of this essay will be a reflection on those questions. This reflection must begin with an extended explanation of the nature of traditional casuistry.

The history of what came to be called casuistry begins in the debates between the Sophists and Plato, but it emerges as a distinctive method of moral reasoning in the work of theologians and canonists of the late Middle Ages. Their purpose was to assist priests in the task of hearing the confessions of penitents, as was required by church law from the early thirteenth century. The method flourished in a large literature produced by Roman Catholic and Anglican theologians in the sixteenth and seventeenth centuries. That literature contained detailed analyses of personal moral problems, such as truth telling, sexual behavior, and honest dealing, as well as discussions of matters of public policy, such as warfare, the duties of rulers, and the acquisition of new territories. For a number of reasons, the popularity of the method began to decline in the late seventeenth century, although it continued to be practiced within Catholic moral theology until the time of Vatican II. It should be noted that this Christian casuistry is paralleled by a Talmudic casuistry, sometimes called pilpul, and by an Islamic casuistry, but these lie outside the scope of our consideration.

12

The word "casuistry" refers to the central feature of this method: namely, the use of cases as the focus and basis of analysis. The books of the classical casuists contain very little of what we would recognize as "ethical theory"; they consist of page after page of cases, brief accounts followed by usually brief commentary. A case, or *casus* (derived from the Latin verb *cadere*, to happen), is literally an event or a happening. It is a story, set in a time and place, with actors having certain qualities who perform describable physical and mental acts. The ancients described a case as "being constructed out of statements about certain persons, places, times, actions, and affairs."[11] There are what is usually called "the circumstances," detailed, from the days of the classical rhetoricians to those of Sherlock Holmes and Rumpole of the Bailey, as "who, what, when, where, why, and how?" But a case in ethics or in law must also contain another essential element: namely, a maxim, a moral rule suited to the story. Thus, a case is made up of circumstances and a maxim or maxims.

Maxims are formulae that give a moral identity to a certain sort of action. In any discussion of killing humans, for example, the maxims will be "Thou shalt not kill," "Do not take innocent life," "Kill only as necessary for self-defense," and so on. Maxims are, quite literally, "pithy"; they express the ethical essence or heart of the matter. Maxims are more modest than principles, since they are, for the most part, not intended to be universal or overarching for morality as such. They are cut to fit the case. In a case that poses a problem of moral interest, several maxims will compete for attention. Thus "Thou shalt not kill" may compete with "An eye for an eye, a tooth for a tooth, a life for a life." Casuistry works at the interpretation and sorting out of maxims in cases. This work is accomplished by three major moves: the first move can be called taxonomic; the second, morphological, and the third, kinetic. The taxonomic move lines up, in comparative order, cases of a similar sort. The Greek word *taxis* refers to drawing up soldiers in a line of battle. In Greek rhetoric, *taxis* (and in Latin, *dispositio*) was that part of the discipline that directed the arrangement of the argument.

13

In casuistry, the taxonomy consists of lining up cases in such a way that competing maxims can be compared in relationship to the circumstances. The leading case in any line may be called the paradigm. *Paradeigma* means, in classical rhetoric, an example and in casuistic method can refer to that case which leads off a series of cases of similar sort. ("Paradigm" does have a history in rhetoric before Thomas Kuhn's appropriation of it in his *Structure of Scientific Revolutions*.) The other cases in the lineup are analogous to the paradigm: that is, similar to it in some respects, yet significantly different.

The primacy of the paradigm case in any lineup is due to its morphology. I use this term, which plays a significant role not in classical rhetoric but rather in biological and botanical science, to describe the structure of an individual case. As just noted, a case consists of circumstances and maxims, but further dissection reveals that there is always more to a case than these apparent parts. Most significantly, there are the arguments that are, as it were, the skeleton of the case. These are what classical rhetoricians called *topoi*, loci, or commonplaces. (The English word "commonplace," which in modern parlance means "platitude," obscures the earlier usage, which translated the Latin and Greek counterparts in the discipline of rhetoric.)

The rhetorical commonplace or topic was at the heart of the discipline of rhetoric itself. Commonplaces are the invariant patterns of reasoning that underlie any practical discourse; they comprise forms of reasoning about common topics, such as comparison (similarity, difference, and degree), relationship (cause and effect, antecedent and consequent, contraries and contradictions), possible, impossible, and improbable, past and future, and the like. The classical rhetoricians noted that no argument could be made without reference to such common topics and that the arguments made about them had an invariant structure. For example, if the case is about killing, it must necessarily invoke causality, and when it does it must do so in certain invariant ways that designate cause in relation to effect. Every criminal lawyer knows these ways, and every aficionado of mysteries can detect fallacies in their use.

In practical reasoning, the common topics take shapes that differ somewhat from their shape in formal logic. This is due in part to their being embedded in a case rather than being idealized. Also, their goal is to produce a probable conclusion rather than an apodictic one. The layout of the argument in practical reasoning will take the form of the assertion of a claim made against the ground of some facts (the circumstances) and in the light of a warrant (the maxim), but open to rebuttals arising from different maxims and leading to a probable conclusion. This form of reasoning is detailed in *The Abuse of Casuistry* and, more comprehensively, in Toulmin's earlier work, *The Uses of Argument*.[12] It is now possible to explain the order of the lineup of cases. The paradigm case, in any segment of moral behavior, will be that case in which one maxim is the only reasonable one to maintain, in the sense that no other maxim can prevail as a rebuttal. By its very nature, the paradigm case is one in which the circumstances are simple and straightforward, and in which the presumptive nature of the claim is overpowering. It is an obvious, open-and-shut case. It is also one in which "any reasonable person" would recognize the right or wrong, or "no reasonable person" would object or doubt the dominance of that maxim for that case. Thus, the deliberate, unprovoked killing of one human being by another, as in a drive-by shooting, is a case in which "Thou shalt not kill" is clearly the only relevant maxim; no other, except those relevant to diminished capacity, could be seriously considered as rebuttal.

For the third step in casuistic thinking, we appropriate the term "kinetics," an invention of classical physics and unknown to classical rhetoric. The term expresses the movement of casuistry from the known to the unknown. Casuistry moves from the paradigms through the analogous cases by asking whether the different circumstances justify the admission of a maxim other than the one appropriate to the paradigm. For example, do the circumstances of the Goetz case—the threatening attitude of several black youths in the dangerous setting of a New York subway car—justify the claim that shooting them was self-defense? The taxonomies will usually consist of familiar maxims facing increasingly complex but still familiar circumstances. However, at a certain point, unprecedented circumstances might appear; then the relevance of the maxims that had been useful previously in that line of cases will be challenged. In classical casuistry, the ethics of taking interest on loans, the so-called problem of usury, is a fascinating history of kinetics.[13] In modern medical ethics, the invention of life-support technologies and the development of biotechnology represent unprecedented circumstances that familiar maxims of medical ethics had never previously faced.

The kinetic of casuistry consists of examining the new or unprecedented circumstances in light of the paradigm and more familiar analogies. The casuist will seek to discover precisely where the circumstances depart from the more familiar analogies. In some, the unprecedented may be nothing more than a particularly dramatic novelty that does not, under close examination, deserve to be denoted a genuinely unprecedented case. The morphology of the earlier cases suffices to describe the moral features of the case. Many of the new reproductive technologies are of this sort. The dramatic technique of in vitro fertilization makes the case appear unprecedented, because the technique certainly is. However, the actual cases of surrogacy or artificial insemination depart in morally relevant ways but little from precedent analogies such as adoption and baby selling. On the other hand, sex change technology does pose genuinely new cases, for the determination on which all of sexual ethics rests—namely, persistence of sexual identity—is abolished.[14]

The kinetics of casuistry represent that function of classical rhetoric called invention. The first task of the rhetorician was to discover the arguments that would make the case most clearly and forcefully. Cicero's *De Inventione* (*On Discovery*), the most renowned of all treatises in rhetoric, is a book about "discovery of valid or seemingly valid arguments that will render one's case plausible."[15] It is this function that leads one of rhetorics' staunchest modern defenders, Richard McKeon, to describe the commonplace as "a heuristic device by which issues that have never been considered before suggest distinctions and relations to be examined in search of a solution . . . the place in which the certainties of the familiar are brought into contact with the transformation of innovation."[16]

It should be clear from this account that traditional casuistry involved much more than "the situation." The case itself is situation in the sense of circumstances and maxims, but the case implies a set of arguments relevant to the situation (the commonplaces) and is itself situated in a taxonomy of cases. Every case presented within traditional casuistry stands within a context of argument and other relevantly similar cases (paradigm and analogy). This being so, we can begin to discern the difference between casuistry and situationism.

A case is a step removed from actuality; it is a conceptualization of experience rather than experience. A case does, indeed, refer to real persons acting and thinking about doing certain sorts of actions in certain circumstances. It does refer to certain relevant maxims that are, in cases of ethical interest, in apparent conflict. But all these are abstractions from actual experience— not remote abstractions, as are theories and principles, but proximate abstractions, needing to be filled out by the actual experience of actual agents.

"Situation" refers to that actual experience. It describes an actual agent, with a name, personal history, private concerns, and interests, living in a moment in which reflection, decision, and action are to be carried out, with definite effects on other persons and things. Situation is not a conceptualization or an abstraction, but a reference to the unique individual in the unique moment. The word "situation" is an apt one; it pictures a person standing in a particular place, on a certain day, and at a particular moment, surrounded by other persons and objects. A decision about a course of action must be made in this very situation.[17] One is reminded of Martin Luther's words, uttered at a fateful moment in Western history: "Here I stand. I cannot do otherwise."

The traditional casuists recognized the situation (they did not use the term, however, in this sense) as the existential setting for choice, the intimate act of conscience, guided by the virtue of prudence. No formulation of a case, however detailed, could capture the reality of the situation as such. That reality was captured only in the experience of the moral agent. In that reality the agent's responsibility was constituted. Only the agent, then, could know his own innocence or guilt. Thus in the Catholic practice of confession that generated casuistry, the agent judged himself sinful and confessed his sin to the priest; the priest did not accuse the agent. The agent's own repentance, of which the priest's absolution was the ecclesiastic acknowledgment, effected innocence.

The case, however, helped penitent and priest to comprehend the situation. The situation, though radically personal, was a situation of a certain sort, capable of being given a name, described, and compared to other situations. Even though the situation was irreducibly singular, it was not ineffable; it could be talked about by agent and priest and evaluated, not as an irreducibly personal act of conscience but as an instance of an act of a certain kind. Thus, by moving to a first level of abstraction above the irreducibly and ineffably personal, a conversation about the morality of choice could take place. This conversation was not about the act of conscience itself but about the case of conscience that most closely approximated the personal act.[18]

The difference, then, between the case and the situation is notable. The case puts the situation into its moral context; it allows judgments to be made both by looking toward the moral taxonomy of the problem and by looking into the intimate conditions of personal life. The cases provide a middle ground between principles and conscience. They present sufficiently rich detail of circumstance to allow an agent to formulate moral options. This conjunction of case and conscience prevents the judgment of conscience from degenerating into "mere personal preference," for it adds to preference the critical dimensions of the case. It allows the agent to measure his or her preferences against the typical circumstances of agent and action and to make a moral discrimination about whether his or her situation differs significantly. A good casuistry inhibits laxism, not because the agent may, in the long run, yield to his or her preferences but because it puts up the concrete barriers of cases before the rush of preferences. The cases allow the agent to say, "Yes, I should do it, but I won't" or "No, I shouldn't, but I will" or "Yes or no, I will, I won't."

The ancient accusation of laxism (which tainted casuistry) and the modern accusation of relativism (which plagues situationism) seem synonymous but are actually different in an important respect. Lax casuistry consisted in the ease with which a competing maxim was admitted as a rebuttal of the ruling maxim in the paradigm case. In situationism, relativism consists in the readiness to make an exception of one's own situation from the norms that usually or generally would govern the situation. In casuistry, the question was, "What are the rational criteria that should be observed when proposing a shift of maxims within the taxonomy of paradigm and analogy?" For the situationist, the question is, "What motive and what consequences license me to exempt myself from the usually or generally right behavior?"

These two questions come together in the question, "How does the presumption of a personal exemption attain the status of a rebuttal?" In problematic personal dilemmas, a man or woman may suppose that the general rule does not apply, in his or her circumstances, but be reluctant to extend the exemption to others or to everyone. This situation, the person may say, is quite different. Even if the exemption were broadened to everyone in the exact situation, it would really apply to no one else, because no one else is or ever will be in the exact same situation. Situations are, as we noted, unique.

An exemption that applies only to the singular agent in the unique situation obviously escapes ethical analysis; it cannot be examined at the level of rational discourse but remains "deep in the heart" of the agent, who "knows" he or she is right—or wrong. Ethics would ask, "Can this personal exemption be grounded in a maxim and urged with sufficient rational force to rebut the ruling maxims?" What sort of argument moves a personal exemption to the status of a rebuttal? When such a move succeeds, a new case is formed in the taxonomy, a case in which the ruling maxim of the paradigm cedes to another maxim. For example, in the taxonomy of cases about human killing, the maxim "Thou shalt not kill" successfully rules a wide range of circumstances but cedes to the maxim "A person has a right to defend his or her own life" as circumstances begin to suggest aggression, attack, threat. Then, the formulation of the maxim in cases close to the paradigm in terms such as "Thou shalt not kill unless in self-defense" shifts to "killing in self-defense is permissible except . . . "

An inoffensive and unprotected black man was beaten to death by skinheads. This case represents the paradigm in the taxonomy of human killing: It is thoroughly immoral. Claims of personal exemption from the maxim prohibiting killing are not allowed to rebut that maxim. Should the skinheads assert that they do not like blacks, or that blacks are taking over the city, or that black persons threaten the white race or white supremacy, we will dismiss such pleas for exemption. In the Bernard Goetz case, in which a white man shot several black men who appeared to him as threatening muggers, we listen to, and evaluate, the claim of self-defense. Self-defense is a maxim that can stand validly as a candidate to rebut the prohibition of killing; personal dislike or racial ideology is not.

The question of interest for ethics is why some maxims should qualify as rebuttals and others not. In casuistry, two approaches to this question are possible (a third way, the effort of formal philosophy initiated by Kant, of seeking the ground of obligation of "the maxim on which I choose to act," falls beyond our present scope). First, we may examine the sociocultural institution that stands behind the taxonomy and inquire how that institution is affected by the admission of certain maxims. Those institutions—such as protection of life and limb, acquisition and transfer of property, communication of ideas and information, sexual practices—have a complex internal structure that is strengthened and preserved or undermined and destroyed by the admission of certain maxims. Too many, too radical, or too idiosyncratic rebutting cases will subvert the institution. Granting that institutions are usually in need of reform and sometimes of revolution, in general they stand as background for the taxonomy of cases and cannot tolerate the weight of a multitude of rebuttals. When rebuttals do begin to accumulate, the institution is—and perhaps should be—under threat. This approach calls for a view of morality as a constitutive element of interpersonal, social, and cultural reality. While the casuist can comment on these issues, they pertain more properly to the work of moral philosophy and moral theology at its highest and broadest.

The other approach to the admission of rebuttals is at the level of the cases themselves. Why, in this case, should we listen to a plea for exemption from the usual? First, because the plea is formulated in a familiar and accepted way: that is, it has long had a place in, and is widely recognized as part of, the taxonomy. It is not strange for an intruder (though intruders can, over time and through debate, become familiar). So a plea of self-defense deserves a hearing; a plea of dislike or racial ideology does not. Second, the circumstances that fit a plea must be recognizable: in self-defense, a person must be the object of violent aggression and should not have provoked that aggression.

Casuistry is now moving on its own ground, what Pascal disdainfully called "the interpretation of circumstances." In such interpretation, an almost quantitative element enters in: one must ask, "How violent? how provocative?" The relative strength of aggressor and victim will be compared; the vigor of the defensive action in relation to that of the attack will be assessed; the seriousness of harm done and harm avoided will be evaluated. In the traditional casuistry of self-defense, these issues were summed up in the maxim "Defense should be limited to what is necessary to repel the attack" (*salvato moderamine inculpatae tutelae*). The Goetz case represents a debate over these "quantitative" matters. In all casuistry, the how-much, how-long, how-many questions are crucial. They are crucial because it is only in light of the answers that the presumed exception can be counted as rebuttal. As in the former approach, the ultimate question is about the extent to which certain sorts of rebuttals undermine a fundamental social institution, but the casuist rarely needs to ask this question explicitly; it will usually be sufficient to review these "quantitative" features of the circumstances and distinguish the "weighty" from the "trivial."

Unquestionably, some subjectivity enters into such a judgment. Casuists, like all other humans, are of varied moral temper—some inclined to severity, others to lenience.

However, the subjectivity was controlled from several directions. The logic of the taxonomy urged the casuist to move cautiously and warned against abrupt departures from the paradigms and analogies. Also, the scrutiny of colleagues encouraged the casuist to be cautious, for the casuists constantly criticized each other's resolution of cases. Finally, the casuist was aware that the resolution would influence the advice given by counselors, for whom the casuist wrote, to many seeking moral counsel. The slippery slope was not a logical or conceptual problem but the prospect of an avalanche of poor advice spread abroad. Thus laxity, while always a possibility and occasionally a reality, was contained on many sides.

These restraints are relaxed in situationism. The individual's supposition that his or her case is unique and that the maxim under which the individual proposes to act is justified, in these circumstances, does not hang on a taxonomy of carefully defined analogous cases. Rather, the problem is posed as the application of a very general principle to a quite particular case, and the principle is viewed as so remote as to be irrelevant. The individual is not surrounded by critical colleagues ready to point out flaws in reasoning. In the modern world, ethical discourse is often exclusively internal to the agent, who turns the problem over in his or her mind but may not expose it to the critical judgment of other prudent persons. Finally, the effect of this decision on many others who may distort what the agent has conscientiously considered is discounted because the agent perceives his or her situation as unique.

Casuistry and situationism are, then, alike in many respects, but the differences should not be ignored. Casuistry and situationism both respect the conscientious judgment of unique persons in unique situations. But for the casuist, the situation is framed by cases that approach it, illuminate it, and challenge it. The casuist asks the agent what it is about the personal situation that justifies a departure from the closest analogies. If the answer is, "Because I want to, or like to," no ethical answer has been given. Any other answer can be subjected to review in light of the taxonomy, and in light of the circumstances, and a judgment made about the "weight" of the reasons. In good casuistry, the relativism is a relationship to the taxonomy and to the social institutions that lie behind the taxonomy. In situationism, the relativism is the relation of the choice to the preferences, needs, and character of the agent. Undoubtedly, both relationships are indelible parts of the moral life; they should never be put asunder. When joined together, they procreate an ethics inheriting both a sensitivity to the existential moments of decision and an appreciation of the essential location of those moments in the moral history of the culture.

Notes

1. Albert R. Jonsen and Stephen E. Toulmin, *The Abuse of Casuistry* (Berkeley and Los Angeles: University of California Press, 1988).
2. Pope Pius XII, *Acta Apostolicae Sedis* 44 (1952), 413–419; *AAS* 46 (1954), 673–619.
3. Harvey Cox, *The Situation Ethics Debate* (Philadelphia: Westminster Press, 1968).
4. Joseph Fletcher, *Situation Ethics*.
5. Blaise Pascal, *The Provincial Letters*, tr. by A. J. Krailsheimer (Baltimore: Penguin Books, 1967), XI, 170.
6. J. C. King, "The Inadequacy of Situation Ethics," *Thomist* 34 (1970), 423–437.
7. Pascal, *Provincial Letters*, VI, 91.
8. E. Hamel, "Valeur et limites de la casuistique," *Loi naturelle et loi du Christ* (Paris: Desclée de Brouwer, 1964); J. Fuchs, "Morale théologie et morale de situation," *Nouvelle Revue Théologique* 76 (1954), 1075; John C. Ford and Gerald Kelly, *Contemporary Moral Theology, I* (Philadelphia: Westminster Press, 1958).

9. Fletcher, *Situation Ethics*, 29–30, 146–150; "What's in a Rule? A Situationist's View," in Gene H. Outka and Paul Ramsey, *Norm and Context in Christian Ethics* (New York: Charles Scribner's Sons, 1968), 336; "The New Look in Christian Ethics," *Harvard Divinity School Bulletin* (Oct. 1959), 10; *Situation Ethics*, 30–31.

10. Fletcher, *Situation Ethics*, 19.

11. Jonsen and Toulmin, *Abuse of Casuistry*, 75–87, 131–136.

12. Stephen E. Toulmin, *The Uses of Argument* (Cambridge: Cambridge University Press, 1969).

13. Jonsen and Toulmin, *Abuse of Casuistry*, ch. 9.

14. Ibid., ch. 16.

15. Cicero, *De Inventione* (Cambridge, Mass.: Harvard University Press, 1976), I, 7, p. 19.

16. Richard P. McKeon, *Rhetoric: Essays in the Invention and Discovery* (Woodbridge, Conn.: Ox Bow Press, 1987), 59, 35.

17. Karl Rahner, "The Question of a Formal Existential Ethics," *Theological Investigations II* (Baltimore: Helicon Press, 1963).

18. Hamel, "Valeur."

Fletcher the Matchmaker
or
Pragmatism Meets Utilitarianism

MARY FAITH MARSHALL

IN 1959, Joseph Fletcher addressed the commencement meeting of the Harvard Divinity School alumni, where he discussed the ethics of contextual or situational decision making in a talk entitled "The New Look in Christian Ethics."[1] During this lecture, Fletcher outlined six propositions that, by his estimation, comprised the fundamentals of Christian conscience. He developed these propositions in greater detail at the presentation of the Easter Bedell Lectures at Kenyon College's Bexley Hall, in 1963, and during a visiting professorship at the International Christian University in Tokyo, where he taught from 1963 to 1964.

Paul Meacham, an editor at The Westminster Press, was present at Fletcher's address to the Harvard alumni and in 1965 asked him to capture his remarks in a small book that could be marketed to "intelligent laymen" as well as to clergy. Fletcher agreed to try and began the book on June 29, 1965.

A little over a month later, Fletcher sent the completed manuscript to Meacham. *Situation Ethics* was published in the spring of 1966 and became an immediate best-seller. Fletcher subsequently referred to the book as his "fat pamphlet" and dreamed of someday revising and expanding it, giving it the full treatment that he felt it merited.

Three best-sellers appeared in that decade of turmoil. John Robinson's *Honest to God* in 1965, Harvey Cox's *Secular City* in 1965, and mine in 1966. Their reception was prompt, the discussion hearty, and approval mixed. I still remember the three of us talking about it in a cellar pub in Fleet Street in London in 1968. We were agreed that the excitement was not due so much to the books themselves as to "something out there" that responded when the button was pushed.[2]

The New Morality: A Historical Perspective

In 1952, Pope Pius XII derisively coined a novel locution, "the new morality," thus endowing a burgeoning theological perspective (to which he was vehemently opposed) with a formal identity![3] The new morality, advocated by an international cadre of Christian theologians of various stripes and creeds, represented the rejection of traditional, legalistic morality in favor of a contextual, personalistic morality. Other contemporaneous designations for this set of positions included such varied terms as "existential ethics," "contextual ethics," "antinomianism," and "situationalism," reflecting widely divergent perceptions regarding the nature of the new morality.

Central Themes of the New Morality

In his excellent paper "The History and Literature of 'The New Morality,'" Edward LeRoy Long outlines its central themes:

1. This approach to ethical decision seems, in the first place, to acknowledge that the claim of the person who stands in the concrete situation, either as recipient or dispenser of neighbor-love, is greater than the claim of any abstract conception of the right.

2. A second important aspect of the new morality is its willingness to make common cause with the moral practices of its culture. It regards the moral changes that are taking place in our time as more to be welcomed and transformed than to be resisted or reversed.

3. Yet a third feature of the "new morality" is its preoccupation with method. This may not be a self-conscious preoccupation nor a matter of deliberate attention, but who can read the literature of the movement without being struck with this characteristic locus of concern?[4]

The Progenitors

Both critics and supporters of the new morality agree that there is not much about it that is truly new. Harvey Cox, for example, maintains that its tenets reach back as far as the beginnings of morality itself.[5] Some, such as Joseph Fletcher, place its origins squarely in the classical Christian tradition of Western Christian morals.[6] Others establish its roots in the Reformation theology of Luther and his contemporaries.

In the 1940s and 1950s, a new movement began among the continental theologians Emil Brunner, Karl Barth, and Dietrich Bonhoeffer for a critical examination of the Reformation belief in justification by faith.[7] Their neo-Reformation critiques were closely allied to the issues of religious legalism and philosophical rationalism, and they provided the primary content for the emerging "new morality." Barth (in his *Church Dogmatics*, especially volume II/2) and Bonhoeffer (in his *Ethics*) were progenitors of the contextualist tradition, and future debate was defined in terms of a new dichotomy: principles (or norms) versus context. Bonhoeffer stated in his *Ethics* that "principles are only tools in God's hands, soon to be thrown away as unserviceable."[8] Brunner, in *Man in Revolt,* devoted an entire chapter to the concept of personality ("The Unity of Personality and Its Decay"), addressing such problems as the divided personality as a consequence of the fall of man, and of the subsequent religious and ethical legalism that ensued from the severance of responsibility from love.[9]

American theologians did not lag far behind in approaching these issues. However, their ideas would not achieve full impact in religious circles until the early 1960s. In 1951, Nels Ferré argued against the central place of rational autonomy in Christian ethics in his essay "Theology and Ethics."[10] Paul Lehmann's paper, "The Foundation and Pattern of Christian Behavior" (1953), received the widest attention that any American treatment of contextual ethics had heretofore enjoyed.[11] Lehmann embraced *koinonia* ethics, or non-rule contextualism.

The new morality was by no means confined to the Protestant tradition. Post-World War II Catholic theologians such as Bernard Haring,[12] Josef Pieper,[13] and Karl Rahner[14] espoused a modified "situational morality" in opposition to the traditional Catholic natural law ethic. Their approach to situationalism was less strident than that of their Protestant counterparts, as they sought a theological marriage between principlism and situationalism.

The Protestant theologian Joseph Sittler argued that Christ's teachings transcended principlism in his essay "The Structure of Christian Ethics" (1958).[15] In 1959, Joseph Fletcher maintained that love was the absolute norm in Christian ethics and argued for situational rather than prescriptive moral decision making.[16] Fletcher approached ethics methodologically rather than systematically because he found no attempt in the Gospel account of Jesus' teachings to develop a system of ethics. He argued that by emphasizing the priority of human need over the moral law, Jesus placed himself in the situationist camp. For Fletcher, the claim to know what God's will is in a situation was presumptuous, thus denying any faith claim that carries cognitive certitude. Jesus Christ is the model of what love means and demands. He personifies agape and is the ideal by which our moral behavior is to be judged.

Fletcher's method is empirical, based on pragmatic assumptions, and he is suspicious of any statement that involves a priori assertions. He echoes Karl Popper's tenet that nonfalsifiable propositions have no place in ethical debate. Faith claims do not provide a basis for moral judgments. His stance is antitheological and antimetaphysical, rejecting any search for "essences," and he chooses a personalistic perspective to describe his philosophical frame of reference of the Christian faith. He does, however, believe in a moral order that is "objectively existent," that applies to individuals and to the law of the community; he describes this position as "ethical realism": "It is this writer's conviction that there is a moral order; that we seek it but we do not make it."[17]

> My rejection of the doctrinaire and the dogmatic bore its fruit in my best-seller, *Situation Ethics*. . . . Its thesis was set forward within the context of Christian rhetoric, but situation ethics as a theory of moral action is, of course, utterly independent of Christian presuppositions or beliefs. . . .
>
> My main principle, that concern for human beings should come before moral rules, and that particular cases and situations are more determinant of what we ought to do than "universal" norms are, was applauded in the helping professions (medicine, social work, public administration, clinical psychology, and so on) but generally condemned by Christians, Jews, and Muslims—most of all by the orthodox ones.
>
> After all, with an absolute God, his word revealed and his will eternal, how could relativity in ethics get anywhere with them? I find it significant, however, that the book was attacked just as fiercely in Marxian journals, such as *Trud* in Moscow and *Science and Society* in America.[18]

The year 1963 was a banner one for contextual and relational ethics, witnessing the publication of Paul Lehmann's *Ethics in a Christian Context*,[19] and H. Richard Niebuhr's posthumous work, *The Responsible Self*.[20]

Anglican bishop John A. T. Robinson published his groundbreaking book *Honest to God* that same year.[21] Robinson espoused the same form of act-agapism over against rule-agapism (locutions coined by William Frankena) as did Fletcher. However, like many of his counterparts in the Roman Catholic tradition, Robinson was unwilling to embrace a full dichotomy between norm and context:

I believe that the "old" and the "new morality" (in any sense in which I am interested in defending the latter) correspond with two starting-points, two approaches to certain perennial polarities in Christian ethics, which are not antithetical but complementary. Each begins from one point without denying the other, but each tends to suspect the other of abandoning what it holds most vital because it reaches it from the other end.[22]

Contemporaneous Critiques

The new morality movement generated a fire storm of reaction from both supporters and critics. Many detractors condemned the progenitors of the new morality for abandoning principles and rules, along with judgment and culture, and questioned the methodological practicalities of the movement's central themes.

One of the earliest condemnations of the contextualist approach came from within the Roman Catholic Church. Pope Pius XII, in an allocution to the Fédération Mondiale des Jeunesses Féminines Catholiques, was unequivocal in his censure:

The distinctive mark of this morality is that it is in fact in no way based on universal moral laws, for instance, on the Ten Commandments, but on the real and concrete conditions or circumstances in which one must act, and according to which the individual conscience has to judge and choose. . . . This personal view spares man from having at every instant to consider whether the decision to take is in conformity with the paragraphs of the law, or with the canons of abstract norms and regulations; it protects him from the hypocrisy of a pharisaical faithfulness to the law; it protects him as much from pathological scrupulousness as from levity or the lack of conscience, because it makes the entire responsibility before God rest personally upon the individual Christian. So speak those who are preaching the "new morality."[23]

Protestant theologians such as Paul Ramsey were equally strident in their denouncements:

Theologians today are simply deceiving themselves and playing tricks with their readers when they pit the freedom and ultimacy of *agapē* (or covenant-obedience, or *koinonia*, or community, or any other primary theological or ethical concept) against rules, without asking whether *agapē* can and may or must work through rules, and embody itself in certain principles which are regulative for the guidance of practice.[24]

Ramsey saw biblical authors as founding their ethics in the nature and activity of God. This was in direct contrast to what he saw as secular emphases on ethics as a product of social evolution or as general assertions about human values. Ramsey proposed that our interest in rules should be based on an appreciation of acts in themselves, and he rejected any kind of teleological or goal-aspiring ethics. God, for Ramsey, calls man to obedient love; therefore, the Christian response to God's demands is not isolated in situational decisions but is grounded in a tradition of action and faith. Ramsey thus moves from general ethical statements regarding past and present meaning of obedience to love. Christian love, for Ramsey, is deontological. The motivation behind a loving act is not evaluated in terms of what it achieves. Ramsey suggests that Christian love is expressed in actions of neighbor love in contrast to loving mankind in general and no one individual in particular. For Ramsey, situation or contextual ethics is a form of "selfish sociability" that misconstrues the meaning of selfless love indicated in the New Testament.[25]

Other critics, such as Bernard Meland, were concerned that proponents of the new morality were attempting to secularize Christianity and that their antiauthoritarian posture would culminate in a radically subjectivist (or purely relativistic) ethos:

One thought that has troubled me in pondering the course of the present concern to secularize Christianity, and now the church's response to the moral life, is that its advocates seem to reflect the same romanticist attitude toward people outside the churches that motivated many earlier liberals and modernists.

In their view they are people with whom alert churchmen and theologians must identify themselves. Their ways must be our ways. What is not meaningful to them or usable by them must be discarded. Christian faith must be streamlined to accord with the energetic and practical bent of mind that characterizes the modern person absorbed in the restrictive routines of the technological era, or in the swift-moving sophisticated life of public figures and the professional intellectuals. Is this not trading one mode of conformity for another, being acquiescent to the demands and conditions of a relativistic ethos instead of being puppets in the hands of an absolutistic and authoritarian church?[26]

James Gustafson, who aligned himself early on with the contextual school,[27] would later characterize the context versus principles dichotomy as "misplaced." From his perspective, the contextualist waters had become unalterably muddied by an overabundance of theorists whose positions were often unrecognizable in terms of their similarities. In his now-classic paper "Context Versus Principles: A Misplaced Debate in Christian Ethics," Gustafson maintained that

the debate is no longer a fruitful one. The umbrella labeled "contextualism" has become so large that it now covers persons whose views are as significantly different from each other as they are different from some of the defenders of "principles."[28]

The Central Claims of Situation Ethics

Joseph Fletcher grounds his ethics in the Christian understanding of agape predicated on the faith assertion that "'God is love' and thence by logic's inference to the value assertion that love is the highest good."[29] Such love is person centered; Fletcher finds the theological justification for this love in the conviction that God is personal. He sees man as made in the image of God; hence persons are of supreme and intrinsic value and are "the first-order concern in ethical choices."[30] His

Christology emerges in the affirmation that we understand love "in terms of God as seen in Christ. . . . Faith working through love" is the essence of Christian ethics.[31]

In *Situation Ethics*, as in *Morals and Medicine*, Fletcher cites Martin Buber as representing the full implication, for all human relationships, of this understanding of God as person. Love is the ultimate norm, "nonreciprocal, neighbor-regarding— 'neighbor' meaning 'everybody,' even an enemy."[32] In contrast to emotion and mere feeling, love is an attitude and an act of will. We choose to love and are known by our loving acts and in a very real sense we *are* our choices. Love's ethical content is affirmed by equating it with justice in which truly expressed agape is concerned with the "rights" of neighbor and the alleviation of those social conditions that preclude the neighbor's full stature as a person.

Christian love expresses itself in benevolent acts of goodwill. It seeks no rewards; it is loving the unlovable and even the unlikable. "This love," says Fletcher, "is as radical as it is because of its nonreciprocal, noncongenial outreach."[33] The motivation behind such love is neither for our own sake nor for the sake of the other person, but for God's sake. However, love of self, love of God, and love of neighbor are harmonized into a self-realization ethic in which God, neighbor, and self are united in a common bond. What might appear to be contradictory and competing loves are actually complementary.

> For to love God and the neighbor is to love one's self in the right way; to love one's neighbor is to respond to God's love in the right way; to love one's self in the right way is to love God and one's neighbors.[34]

Fletcher's ethical perspective in *Situation Ethics* is epistemological in the sense that it employs a quasi-empirical method. Its pragmatic presuppositions and its method (a modification of Dewey's valuation process) rely on the belief that creative human intelligence employing judgment, decision, and action can construct and achieve new, more positive moral ends.

Fletcher's perspective is informed by two fundamental positions. The first attests to the constancy of his personalist leanings; it holds that concern for human beings supersedes concern for moral rules. The second, and more radical position holds that objective circumstances or situations—not norms—should determine moral action.

> This situational way of looking at value problems, which leaves aside all grandiose and "ultimate" theories of good and evil, took full hold of me at a meeting on social justice held in Geneva by the World Council of Churches. Bishop Brooke Mosley, once my student in Cincinnati, asked me to go. I found their way of looking at social issues in terms of prefabricated doctrines of Christian theology was by now alien and irritating. I could not help but compare it to the humility and exact knowledge I always found in Geneva at the World Health Organization when I'd attend their medical ethics sessions.
>
> My nondoctrinaire approach to problems not only ran me straight athwart religious social ethics but also religious personal ethics too. . . .
>
> In two summary words, I was at last a *humanist situationist—* in matters both personal and social.[35]

Fletcher maintained that the substantive principle of ethical conduct is agape, or loving concern, and its opposite is malice, or indifference, thus eliminating all other universal negatives and positives. He classified his perspective as a neocasuistical method, not an ethical *system*, because system and method were, for him, inherently antithetical. Systems connote rules and prescriptions and are inherently inflexible, whereas methods allow for response to situational variables. Fletcher's method reduces to a simple formula: the imperative (love) combined with the indicative (empirical data) determines the normative (the good thing to do).

By design his methodological thesis did not address the content problem of moral theology. He categorically refused to examine the question of the "content of love," maintaining that such an endeavor could only hinge on prefabricated norms and result in moral legalism.

Fletcher advanced six propositions that provide content for his method. They are:

1. Only one "thing" is intrinsically good: namely, love; nothing else at all.[36]
2. The ruling norm of Christian decision is love: nothing else.[37]
3. Love and justice are the same, for justice is love distributed, nothing else.[38]
4. Love wills the neighbor's good whether we like him or not.[39]
5. Only the end justifies the means; nothing else.[40]
6. Love's decisions are made situationally, not prescriptively.[41]

Four presuppositions provided a framework for his methodological thesis: pragmatism, relativism, positivism, and personalism. Fletcher's return to pragmatism (a philosophical school of thought he had embraced during his undergraduate and graduate years and had subsequently replaced with orthodox Christian theology) represented a rejection of the idea that metaphysics could bridge the gap between doubt and faith.

His method reflects the presupposition of relativity in its "tactics." Values are relative to the situation, nothing is inherently good or evil, with the exception of the absolute norm of agape, and its opposites, malice and indifference.

The situationist avoids words like "never" and "perfect" and "always" and "complete" as he avoids the plague, as he avoids "absolutely." . . . To be relative, of course, means to be relative *to* something. To be "absolutely relative" (an uneasy combination of terms) is to be inchoate, random, unpredictable, unjudgeable, meaningless, amoral—rather in the antinomian mode. There must be an absolute or norm of some kind if there is to be any true relativity. This is the central fact in the normative relativism of a situation ethic.[42]

Situation ethics is grounded in theological positivism in an epistemological sense. It involves a voluntary faith assertion that "'posits' faith in God and *reasons* out what obedience to his commandment to love requires in any situation."[43] Fletcher was careful to point out that secular ethics also involves a leap of faith, in the sense that "any moral or value judgment in ethics, like a theologian's faith proposition, is a *decision*—not a conclusion."[44]

Perhaps the most pervasive assumption in *Situation Ethics* is its personalism, a position that Fletcher first fully explicated in *Morals and Medicine*. For Fletcher, persons are of first-order value. He held strongly that "good derives from the needs of people. . . . Only people can exercise the freedom that is essential in the forum of conscience for decision-making. Only free persons, capable of being 'the responsible self,' can sustain relationship and thereby enter the field of obligation."[45]

While the thought of philosophers such as James, Dewey, Mill, Thomas Browne, and Kant heavily influenced Fletcher's ethical positions, he never engaged in any sophisticated analysis or application of their metaphysics. Fletcher was a synthesizer, not a philosopher. He was adept at appropriating particular components of various philosophical and theological doctrines and fashioning them into a unique conception. He was a creator of positions and perspectives, not theories.

The defining features of his perspective are its pragmatism and its personalism. His other presuppositions, relativism and positivism, follow from these basic constructs. Fletcher holds that value judgments are *decisions*.[46] He borrows Dewey's naturalist conception of ethics, modifies his process of moral deliberation known as "valuation," and adopts his reconstructive social philosophy, which embraces the belief that the human condition can be changed, via the efficacious use of intelligence and choice, and that persons have a responsibility continually to reconstruct their experiences. To do otherwise, Dewey (and subsequently Fletcher) maintains, would be dehumanizing.

Fletcher rejects conventional norms in favor of bringing ethics to bear on specific problems in concrete situations. This approach is contiguous with his earlier rejection (in *Morals and Medicine*) of dealing with ethics on the abstract level, a position informed by the thought of Buber as well as the pragmatists James and Dewey. For Fletcher, moral judgments do not lend themselves to verification, and moral action cannot be derived from factual or descriptive statements.

Fletcher accuses the Western religious tradition (Judaism, Catholicism, and Protestantism) of a legalistic approach to morality and a systematic orthodoxy. Moral absolutes and rigid norms resulted from belief in a supernatural justification of morality. Moral virtue depended on the concept of individual perfection as its ideal; thus the disapprobation of digression from moral norms as inherently sinful. Fletcher considered this legalistic approach to religious ethics to be ultimately depersonalizing. It was antithetical to his cardinal elements of moral decision making: freedom and choice.

The Pragmatist Influence on *Situation Ethics*

William James

More so than that of any other progenitors of the new morality, Fletcher's position turned on the thought of the American pragmatists James and Dewey. His method was pragmatic in that it centered on concreteness, actions, facts, and power. These themes were borrowed directly from William James.

> A pragmatist turns his back resolutely and once for all upon a lot of inveterate habits dear to professional philosophers. He turns away from abstraction and insufficiency, from verbal solutions, from bad a priori reasons, from fixed principles, closed systems, and pretended absolutes and origins. He turns toward concreteness and adequacy, toward facts, toward actions, and toward power.[47]

Fletcher's predisposition toward moral individualism and his dismissal of moral determinism is attributable to James's pragmatist ethics. James held that the unfortunate consequence of a deterministic perspective was moral pessimism. Determinism countered any belief or hope in a causal relationship between one's moral efforts and a more positive future. For James, moral determinism was an ethic of despair and defeat. He posited that our morality depends on the efforts we make as moral agents; we are capable of changing our futures and effecting a better life.

Although the debate between determinists and indeterminists allows for consideration at the metaphysical level (regarding postulations whether prior choices *could* or *could not* have, a priori, been otherwise), neither James nor, subsequently, Fletcher was willing to entertain the argument in these terms. James considered the issue on pragmatic grounds; for him, a belief represented an idea that one was willing to act on, thus allowing for future possibilities. Belief in indeterminism leads to the type of moral optimism evident in Fletcher's earlier work, *Morals and Medicine*. While indeterminism makes neither claims regarding a better future nor predictions as to whether human efforts will result in their chosen goals, it allows for the possibility of effecting change.

The situationist dismissal of absolute moral justifications and its reliance on concrete situations evolved directly from pragmatist ethics. James rejected the idea of a retributive or punishing God, as well as the notion of original sin. He was a fervent advocate of moral individualism. For him, the individual is the central and ultimate focus of value. He conceived of a basic polarity between tough-minded and tender-minded individualism and strove to maintain an equilibrium between the two: tough-minded individualism required grounding ideas in facts; tender-minded individualism called for an appreciation of human values. Morality, being personal, hinges on choice, commitment, and conduct. He contended that individual experience was the sole source of information for moral discourse and that the qualifying characteristics of experience are diversity and change. Thus, any predetermined norm or moral absolute would by necessity be inadequate as a moral guide or determinant of behavior.

Moral individualism requires the individual to shoulder the burden of moral responsibility. This presupposes a belief in free will, an existential leap that confirms one's individual freedom.

John Dewey

In *Reconstruction in Philosophy*, John Dewey attempted to reconstruct ethics within an empirical paradigm. He contended that the social sciences, especially sociology and psychology, were vital components in the examination of value theory. Science, for Dewey, provided the means of ethical analysis. He considered the (empirical) social sciences, in particular, as necessary conditions for the efficacy of moral decision making, since they allow us to predict the consequences of a particular moral choice or course of action.

Dewey looked to the situation for the resolution of a problem and saw the rationality of the solution as key. He proposed evaluating the context of a particular problem in scientific terms.

Now the simple fact of the case is that any inquiry into what is deeply and inclusively human enters perforce into the specific area of morals. It does so whether it intends to and whether it is even aware of it or not. When "sociological" theory withdraws from consideration of the basic interests, concerns, the actively moving aims, of a human culture on the ground that "values" are involved and that inquiry as "scientific" has nothing to do with values, the inevitable consequence is that inquiry in the human area is confined to what is superficial and comparatively trivial, no matter what its parade of technical skills. But, on the other hand, if and when inquiry attempts to enter in critical fashion into that which is human in its full sense, it comes up against the body of prejudices, traditions, and institutional customs that consolidated and hardened in a pre-scientific age. For it is tautology, not the announcement of a discovery or of an inference, to state that morals, in both senses of the word, are pre-scientific when formed in an age preceding the rise of science as now understood and practiced. And to be unscientific, when human affairs in the concrete are immensely altered, is in effect to resist the formation of methods of inquiry into morals in a way that renders existing morals—again in both senses— anti-scientific.[48]

Dewey conceived of experience as the primary unit of life; thus his emphasis on the importance of the situation. He rejected the "spectator theory of knowledge" in favor of an epistemological theory that knowledge is a function of experimental manipulation. Dewey posited the type of reconstructed experience known as a "consummation." Experiences are consummated by being reconstructed through the use of intelligence and the application of scientific method. When faced with a problematic situation, one reconstructs the situation by locating its internal problems and constructing a resolution. The internal problems or conflicts in a given situation cause the individual to experience a "felt difficulty" that is the basic prerequisite to inquiry. Once the problems in the situation have been articulated, the hypothesis phase begins, in which one formulates various hypotheses and engages in deductive reasoning to anticipate the consequences of the proposed course of action.

When faced with moral dilemmas or value conflicts, individuals engage in a process of deliberation that Dewey called "valuation." Because situations involving moral problems inherently involve conflicts of value, we cannot appeal to our values to resolve them. We must evaluate the situation or experience empirically, consider the possible choices of action, and imagine their consequences. We then construct the goods (or ends) based on an intelligent outcome appraisal. Intelligent deliberation will result in rational choices; deliberation based on prejudice or ignorance results in irrational choices.

In a recent chapter on Dewey's ethics in *Ethics in the History of Western Philosophy* (1989), James Gouinlock provides a cogent analysis of Dewey's formulation of ethical discourse as scientific. Gouinlock maintains that Dewey's attempt to introduce scientific method into ethics too often receives an undeservedly complex and complicating treatment by its expositors. In basic terms, Dewey placed the situation within a scientific paradigm:

the dependent variable that could be introduced and manipulated, that formed the key to a given outcome, was the basic value or good that one constructed.

> What it means to be scientific in the moral life is really quite simple, but many followers and critics of Dewey have made the crucial mistake of assuming that the scientific dimension is exhaustive of all moral reflection and discourse. To be scientific means, first, that one exercises creative intelligence. . . . Valued events are properties of objective relationships. Hence, like any other event in nature, they are subject to prediction and control. More importantly, values or goods can be deliberately constructed; that is, we may formulate hypotheses that propose specific reconstructions of a given situation. If the hypothesis is more or less accurate, and if we introduce the conditions prescribed by it, then we will transform the situation from problematic to consummatory. This, and only this, is what Dewey means when he speaks of ideas directing conduct. He has no thought of resurrecting a demonstrative process—whether of particular imperatives deduced from generic principles or evaluative statements derived from descriptive. Such reasoning would be precisely to disinter the absolutist logic of the classic tradition.[49]

There are many similarities between the ethical approaches of Dewey and Fletcher. The role that love plays in the situationist's approach to moral problems is analogous to the role that science plays in Dewey's thought. While for Dewey the social sciences were imperative in ethical analysis, Christian love was vital for Fletcher. While Dewey called for a scientific interpretation of the context of a situation, Fletcher called for a theological interpretation in posing the question, "What is God doing?" While the situationists were attempting to differentiate between reason and faith, Dewey was examining the distinction between the empirical "is" and the evaluative "ought."[50]

> The pragmatic-empirical temper of situation ethics . . . calls for a radical reversal of the classic approach. It focuses on cases and

tries experientially, not propositionally, to adduce, not deduce, some "general" ideas to be held only tentatively and lightly. It deals with cases in all their contextual particularity, deferring in fear and trembling only to the rule of love. Situation ethics keeps principles sternly in their place, in the role of advisers without veto power![51]

Perhaps the best theoretical source for understanding Fletcher's position on rules is Dewey's pragmatic ethics. In his discourse on "The Nature of Principles" in *Human Nature and Conduct*, Dewey discusses the status of moral rules from the pragmatist perspective.[52] He posits that to take moral rules as fixed is to shut the door on experience. Because human situations change, rules or principles must also change. Rules, for Dewey, are hypotheses, only justified insofar as they accord with experience. It follows that rules will be revised if they no longer provide satisfactory guidance under changed circumstance, just as the laws of science are modified based on new knowledge or theoretical perspectives.

Dewey maintained that ethics should follow science in criticizing and revising rules in the light of new experiences. Rules are the tools in the process of deliberation, not sacred laws that must be unconditionally obeyed. As tools, rules are to be used, modified, or rejected depending on how they work. Moral rules are merely tentative guides that have worked so far. They are neither fixed in their meaning nor final.

Critique of Situation Ethics

Situation ethics as a method of ethical deliberation is a curious mixture of elements that do and don't work. While none of its independent parts are broken (for they are all borrowed from other traditional theological or philosophical perspectives), the sum of the parts, the synthesis, fails to achieve its end. It fails primarily because its guiding norm lacks content. Without knowing what love means in a given situation, one is hard pressed to determine how to realize it.

Throughout *Situation Ethics*, Fletcher engages in self-contradiction, superficial interpretations, and oversimplifications of complex theological and metaphysical approaches to ethics. His method tries to be and do too many things at once; its attempt to marry consequentialism, pragmatism, and quasi-principlism results in a serious identity crisis.

Fletcher ostensibly rejects prior and external norms in the resolution of ethical problems and demands that ethical situations be appraised as being between persons. Principles, he maintains, are subordinated to circumstances. Situation ethics opposes any norm or content that is prior to the situation. It is inductive in its approach to moral problems, beginning with persons, not principles. Ethical decisions cannot occur before problems, for somehow the context of the problem provides decisions. Fletcher acknowledges no inherent goods or evils (excepting love, malice, and indifference).

"By situational the new morality means a structure of events in which moral solutions are produced out of empirically known situational elements, all of this under the control of the norm of love."[53]

Harvey Seifert in his essay "The Promise and Peril of Contextualism" has outlined three sets of factors that the contextualist brings to bear on ethical decision making: the theological realities (the absolute norm of love), a system of ethical principles, and the sociological data describing the particular situation.[54] Each of these factors brings to light important liabilities in the situationist method.

The norm of absolute love is problematic in its lack of meaning or content. Without some sort of middle axiom or principle to define or lend meaning to a particular situation, one is asked to make an impossible leap of logic, or intuition, from the purely abstract to the particular. Love is, practically speaking, totally ambiguous, in terms of what it means in a concrete situation. Fletcher, Robinson, and others wrongly presume that the abstract concept of agape, neighbor love or Christian love, provides sufficient guidance or meaning to allow one to leap this conceptual chasm. A general concern for the well-being of others is noble, but somehow one must determine by what means this well-being is to be achieved.

There are two problems inherent in this issue. First, one's moral vision is impaired without some a priori guidelines, or illuminators of an ethical problem; lacking such vision, one is not capable of recognizing a moral dilemma when confronted with it. How is a value conflict to be recognized when there is only one overarching value? Next, what factors does one weigh—within the context of the situation—in order to determine the most loving outcome? Radical contextualism, without the presence of middle axioms or principles to serve as moral guidelines, can only allow for an individual to discover by intuition or revelation the goodness that Fletcher maintains is inherent in the act or the decision.

Another crucial factor that enters into ethical decision making is the application of a system of principles. If Fletcher really wants to deny the efficacy of general action guides for moral behavior, he is also denying the similarities that inhere among many situations. He is, in a sense, forcing moral deliberation to be ahistorical, or existential. By so doing, he also risks depersonalizing his method, for he replaces the complex human personality, with its social and biographical values and beliefs, with the abstract good of love or the concrete facts of situations.

To maintain that a given moment or situation contains everything necessary for moral decision making is to deny both its historical and its sociological contexts, which are as valid a part of the situational context as its immediate facts; this denial is also contradictory. One cannot comprehend the full meaning of the situation without one's own prior experience and the prior historical experience of the community.

This is contrary to his contention that the situationist method is somehow neocasuistical. In his diatribe against legalism,[55] Fletcher makes a convincing argument for the need for a casuistical method but maintains that it must be flexible, must respond to what love demands in a particular situation.

Any web thus woven sooner or later chokes its weavers. Reformed and even Conservative Jews have been driven to disentangle themselves from it. Only Orthodoxy is still in its coils. Something of the same pilpul and formalistic complication may be seen in Christian history. With Catholics it has taken the form of a fairly ingenious moral theology that, as its twists and involutions have increased, resorts more and more to a casuistry that appears (as, to its credit, it does) to evade the very "laws" of right and wrong laid down in its textbooks and manuals. Love, even with the most stiff-necked of system builders, continues to plead mercy's cause and to win at least partial release from law's cold abstractions. Casuistry is the homage paid by legalism to the love of persons, and to realism about life's relativities.[56]

Fletcher is perceived by many as too radical in his contextualist method and too firm in his dismissal of principlism. Yet just as he rejects legalism, he also rejects its polar opposite, antinomianism.

This is the approach with which one enters into the decision-making situation armed with no principles or maxims whatsoever, to say nothing of *rules*. In every "existential moment" or "unique" situation, it declares, one must rely upon the situation of itself, *there and then*, to provide its ethical solution.[57]

He attempts to take the middle ground between these two dichotomous positions. "The situationist enters into every decision-making situation fully armed with the ethical maxims of his community and its heritage, and he treats them with respect as illuminators of his problems."[58] However, if love is better served in the situation by abandoning these principles, Fletcher is prepared to do so. Herein lies internal contradiction. Without assigning higher priority to one or the other of conflicting principles or values, how does Fletcher's method work itself out? Without providing normative content, how is love supposed to answer any moral dilemma?

45

Fletcher and his counterparts seem unrealistic in their approach. If a priori principles truly illuminate value conflicts, where is the guiding light when they are suddenly withdrawn? Without them, how can like cases be treated similarly and unlike cases be treated dissimilarly? How does one avoid the risk of treating exceptional cases in a typical fashion—that is, making rules out of exceptions? How can principles be subordinate to circumstances and simultaneously "illuminate" them?

Conversely, how can the objective facts of a situation determine the outcome of moral decisions? In making value judgments, individuals engage in a process that balances internal convictions against external norms. By minimizing the importance of both conscience and external norms, principles, or rules, Fletcher risks allowing the facts of objective situations to dictate moral decisions—a kind of perverse naturalistic fallacy. To consider every situation as totally unique would disallow legislation, policy decisions, the establishment of a social ethic, or any sort of utilitarian calculus.

Fletcher misses an important internal contradiction in his central presuppositions. His positivism (whether theological or secular) is of second-order importance to his pragmatist method. Even if one were to allow for Fletcher's faith assumption that Christian (or neighbor) love is the ultimate prescriptive norm, one is still faced with the problem of recognizing a moral dilemma and discovering what love allows in a given situation.

Ironically, Fletcher made this very observation about the pragmatist school. "Pragmatism of itself yields none of the norms we need to measure or verify the very success that pragmatism calls for!"[59] To solve this problem, one must repair to Dewey's valuation process. Determining what love demands in a given context is still a process of human deliberation, an exercise of human intelligence within a scientific (that is, problem-oriented) framework.

One of the most cogent and frequently voiced criticisms of situation ethics centers on Fletcher's third proposition: that "love and justice are the same, for justice is love distributed."[60] Fletcher argues that his method is utilitarian, that as the love ethic searches seriously for a social policy it must form a coalition with utilitarianism. It takes over from Bentham and Mill the strategic principle of "the greatest good of the greatest number." . . . We need not try to assert some supposed mutual exclusion as between *agapē* and the "happiness" that utilitarians want. All depends upon what we find our happiness in: all ethics are happiness ethics. With hedonists it is one's own pleasure (physical or mental); with neo-Aristotelians it is self-realization; with naturalists it is adjustment, gratification, and survival. Happiness is the pragmatist's *satisfaction*. It is "how you get your kicks." The Christian situationist's happiness is in doing God's will as it is expressed in Jesus' Summary. And his utility method sets him to seeking his happiness (pleasure, too, and self-realization!) by seeking his neighbors' good on the widest possible scale.[61]

This seems directly antithetical to the following statement:

The universal law is that every moral action should be unique and individual, i.e., that it should have in view a concrete living person and not the abstract good. Such is the ethics of love. Love can only be directed upon a person, a living being, and not upon the abstract good.[62]

This internal contradiction in Fletcher's method results from his unhappy attempt to marry a pragmatic method with a utilitarian philosophy. Dewey's ethics received the same criticism, which is surprising in light of its inherently democratic perspective, which makes his ethics consistent with his social philosophy. Richard J. Bernstein has this to say about Dewey's valuation process:

It should also be clear that ethics conceived in this [Dewey's] manner blends into social philosophy. Valuation, like all inquiry, presupposes a community of shared experiences in which there are common norms and procedures, and intelligent valuation is also a means for making such a community a concrete reality. Here, too, ends and norms are clarified, tested, and modified in light of the cumulative experience of the community.[63]

Fletcher was not the antinomian, or even cryptoantinomian, that he was often accused of being. "I personally would adopt nearly all the norms or action-principles ordinarily held in Christian ethics. I refuse, on the other hand, to treat their norms as idols."[64]

Fletcher, however, only partially adopted Dewey's method of moral deliberation. He looked ultimately for differences of quantity in various situational outcomes, while Dewey argued strongly against such a calculus. Instead, Dewey looked to an appraisal of consequences simply as a way of finding meaning in the current situation. He rejected the concept of outcome as legitimate end.

Fletcher, however, sought an act-utilitarian approach, attempting to replace the utilitarians' pleasure principle with agape, looking for "the greatest amount of neighbor welfare for the largest number of neighbors possible."[65] Dewey would have dismissed this agapeic calculus:

> After all, the object of foresight of consequences is not to predict the future. It is to ascertain the meaning of present activities and to secure, so far as possible, a present activity with a unified meaning . . . the problem of deliberation is not to calculate future happenings but to appraise present proposed actions. We judge present desires and habits by their tendency to produce certain consequences. It is our business to watch the course of our action so as to see what is the significance, the import of our habits and dispositions. . . . Every attempt to forecast the future is subject in the end to the auditing of present concrete impulse and habit. Therefore the important thing is the fostering of those habits and impulses which lead to a broad, just, sympathetic survey of situations.[66]

Conclusion

Ultimately, it seems that Fletcher's amalgamated method is too complex, too rich, and too contradictory to result in a successful means of resolving moral conflict. Lacking the mainstays of principles or middle axioms, agape as an absolute norm provides insufficient content for concrete moral action, whether applied from a secular perspective or within the context of traditional Christian theological ethics. Fletcher's deviation from the path of Deweyian reconstruction, his meanderings down the utilitarian trail lead him to fatal internal contradictions in his methodology that preclude successful resolution of the problems of social justice or the application of any neocasuistical approach that he might have supposed was possible. In the end, the whole is less than the sum of its parts.

Take, by way of example, his position on famine relief. In concert with his friend and colleague, the social biologist Garrett Hardin, Fletcher argued that providing aid to starving persons is morally wrong when it will only compound their collective misery by allowing them to procreate and consequently produce more starving persons.

> We must presume that no responsible person would insist on sharing regardless of the consequences, whether in matters of food or anything else. We ought not to enter upon courses of action which foreseeably end in the negation of the good being sought. . . . Could it not be, then, that in some situations in the world the virtue of generosity—in the form of food relief—should be set aside? Are there not places where food relief would result in keeping the starving alive long enough to procreate even more people to starve, without closing the gap between their production of food and their production of hungry bellies—in effect only adding to the numbers of those who die of disease and starvation.[67]

Fletcher calls the idea that something should be shared simply because it is available the "capacity fallacy."[68] Using a utilitarian calculus, he seeks to avoid the greatest amount of suffering and would have us believe that in so doing love would have us withhold aid to those in need. Had he applied a more strictly Deweyian approach, he might have considered any number of other possible solutions to the problem of feeding the hungry. A more empirical view of "the situation" might identify the central problem differently, as one of overpopulation, and could focus possible solutions along the lines of contraception and birth control (or some combination of feeding and contraception).

Implicitly, Fletcher is advocating starvation as a means of birth control. His approach to this problem of distributive justice could have been made more successful by "reconstructing the situation," by defining the problem in different terms, and by conceiving a less rigid and simplistic solution to a complex problem.

Notes

1. Joseph Fletcher, "The New Look in Christian Ethics," *Harvard Divinity School Bulletin* (Oct. 1959). In *Morals and Medicine*, and in a letter to The Westminster Press regarding Paul Meacham, editor of *Situation Ethics*, Fletcher erroneously gives the date of the Harvard Divinity School address as May 1965.

2. Joseph Fletcher, letter sent on request to The Westminster Press regarding Paul Meacham, date unknown; return address University of Virginia School of Medicine.

3. The locution "new morality" was coined by Pope Pius XII on April 19, 1952, in an allocution to the Fédération Mondiale des Jeunesses Féminines Catholiques.

4. Edward LeRoy Long, Jr., "The History and Literature of 'The New Morality,' " *The Pittsburgh Perspective* 3 (Sept. 1966), 4–17. This essay by Long also appears in *The Situation Ethics Debate*, ed. by Harvey Cox (Philadelphia: Westminster Press, 1968), 101–116.

5. Cox, *Situation Ethics Debate*, 9.

6. Joseph Fletcher, *Situation Ethics*, 13.

7. Long, "History," 4–17.

8. Dietrich Bonhoeffer, *Ethics*, tr. by N. H. Smith (New York: Macmillan Co., 1958), 8.

9. H. Emil Brunner, *Man in Revolt: A Christian Anthropology* (Philadelphia: Westminster Press, 1947), 230.

10. Nels Ferré, "Theology and Ethics," *Minutes of the Presbyterian Educational Association of the South*, 1951, 47–77.

11. Paul Lehmann, "The Foundation and Pattern of Christian Behavior," in John A. Hutchison, ed., *Christian Faith and Social Action* (New York: Charles Scribner's Sons, 1959), 93–116.

12. Bernard Haring, *The Law of Christ I* (Westminster, Md.: Newman Press, 1961).

13. Josef Pieper, *Prudence: The First Cardinal Virtue* (New York: Pantheon Books, 1959).

14. Karl Rahner, "On the Question of a Formal Existential Ethics," *Theological Investigations*, vol. 2 (New York: Taplinger Publishing Co., 1964).

15. Joseph A. Sittler, *The Structure of Christian Ethics* (Baton Rouge, La.: Louisiana State University Press, 1958).

16. Fletcher, "New Look in Christian Ethics."

17. Joseph Fletcher, *Morals and Medicine*, xix.

18. Joseph Fletcher, "Memoir of an Ex-Radical" (unpublished, 1983), 24–25.

19. Paul L. Lehmann, *Ethics in a Christian Context* (New York: Harper & Row, Publishers, 1963).

20. H. Richard Niebuhr, The *Responsible Self* (San Francisco: Harper & Row, Publishers, 1963).

21. John A. T. Robinson, *Honest to God* (Philadelphia: Westminster Press, 1963).

22. John A. T. Robinson, *Christian Morals Today* (Philadelphia: Westminster Press, 1964), 10.

23. His Holiness Pope Pius Xll, *L'Osservatore Romano*, April 19, 1952.

24. Paul Ramsey, "Deeds and Rules in Christian Ethics," *Scottish Journal of Theology Occasional Papers*, no. 11 (Edinburgh: Oliver Boyd, 1964).

25. Paul Ramsey, *Basic Christian Ethics* (New York: Charles Scribner's Sons, 1950), 100.

26. Bernard E. Meland, "A New Morality—But to What End?" *Religion in Life*, vol. 35, no. 2 (Spring 1966), 195.

27. James Gustafson, "Christian Ethics and Social Policy," in Paul Ramsey, ed., *Faith and Ethics* (New York: Harper & Brothers, 1957), 119–139.

28. James Gustafson, "Context Versus Principles: A Misplaced Debate

in Christian Ethics," *Harvard Theological Review*, 58, no. 2 (April 1965), 173.

29. Fletcher, *Situation Ethics*, 49.
30. Ibid., 51.
31. Ibid., 49.
32. Ibid., 79.
33. Ibid., 105.
34. Ibid., 114.
35. Fletcher, "Memoir," 26–27.
36. Fletcher, *Situation Ethics*, 57.
37. Ibid., 69.
38. Ibid., 87.
39. Ibid., 103.
40. Ibid., 120.
41. Ibid., 134.
42. Ibid., 43–45.
43. Ibid., 47.
44. Ibid.
45. Ibid., 50–51.
46. Ibid., 47.
47. William James, *Pragmatism* (Longmans, Green & Co., 1907), 51.
48. John Dewey, *Reconstruction in Philosophy* (Boston; Beacon Press, 1948), xxvi–xxvii.
49. James Gouinlock, "Dewey," in *Ethics in the History of Western Philosophy*, ed. by Robert J. Cavalier, James Gouinlock, and James P. Sterba (New York: St. Martin's Press, 1989), 314.
50. Robert L. Cunningham, *Situationism and the New Morality* (New York: Appleton-Century-Crofts, 1970), 45.
51. Fletcher, *Situation Ethics*, 55.
52. John Dewey, "The Nature of Principles," in *Human Nature and Conduct, 1922: The Middle Works of John Dewey: 1899–1924* (Carbondale and Edwardsville, Ill.: Southern Illinois University Press, 1988), 164–170.
53. Elton M. Eenigenberg, "How New Is the New Morality?" in *The Situation Ethics Debate*, ed. by Harvey Cox (Philadelphia: Westminster Press, 1968), 216.
54. Harvey Seifert, "The Promise and Peril of Contextualism," in *The Situation Ethics Debate*, 225–226.
55. Fletcher, *Situation Ethics*, 18–19.
56. Ibid., 19.

57. Ibid., 22.
58. Ibid., 26.
59. Ibid., 42.
60. Ibid., 87.
61. Ibid., 95–96.
62. Joseph Fletcher, "Reflection and Reply," in Cox, *The Situation Ethics Debate*, 255.
63. Richard J. Bernstein, "John Dewey," in *The Encyclopedia of Philosophy*, ed. by Paul Edwards (New York: Macmillan Publishing Co., 1967), 384–385.
64. Fletcher in Cox, *Situation Ethics Debate*, 252.
65. Fletcher, *Situation Ethics*, 95.
66. John Dewey, *Human Nature and Conduct*, 143–144.
67. Joseph Fletcher, "Feeding the Hungry: An Ethical Appraisal," in *Soundings*, 59, no. 1 (Spring 1976), 54.
68. This term was first coined in *The Ethics of Genetic Control: Ending Reproductive Roulette* (New York: Doubleday & Co., Anchor Books, 1974), 5–6.

PART TWO

Memoir of an Ex-Radical

JOSEPH FLETCHER

WHEN I WAS NINE my parents separated and my mother decided she wanted to leave New York and go back home with
her children, my sister and me. Actually, we were then living in
the Oranges—over in Jersey. Home for her was West Virginia,
and that was how I came to live there for a growing-up decade.
A couple of years or so after we went down there, word came
that my father had died.

It's too bad that I know so little about my father, Joseph
pére. His father's name was Edward. He had two uncles: one
was Joseph, a professor of histology, the other (name not
known) was said to be "the most popular barkeep in Dublin."
Edward married Annie O'Reilly of County Meath about 1850,
and they came on their honeymoon to central New York, to
Utica, where they settled. They had several children, Joseph
being perhaps the youngest. My feeling always was that I should
not try to look them up—that it wasn't wanted.

My father was a sick man when my parents broke up; my
mother was always tight-lipped or at least laconic about it, and
early I learned to stay away from the subject. She once said
something about his being sick not only in his heart but in his

soul. One thing I'm pretty sure of: lapsed Catholic though my father was, his family did everything they could to wean him away from a wife who was a Protestant heretic and therefore unacceptable; they were angry because she (and he too) would not agree to bring their children up as Catholics. Although he did not really leave his family, he did, nonetheless, let them leave him. I don't know if there was an actual legal divorce, but I doubt it; I think his death settled all that.

He was a man of average height, I would judge. Dark brown hair and eyes and mustachios. I'd like to have seen him in his Rough Rider uniform; he went to Cuba with Teddy Roosevelt, although somehow I have the impression that he did not take part in the charge up San Juan Hill. He took me pole fishing a few times in the Morris Canal in north Jersey, and he liked to go fishing with other men when the "smelts were running" out beyond the Narrows and Sandy Hook. He commuted daily to Manhattan on the Lackawanna, crossing the Hudson on the Weehawken ferry. I can remember his taking me to see the new Woolworth Building (then a skyscraper), on a New Year's morning when the area was nearly deserted, and to a high place somewhere along the harbor to watch the Atlantic fleet steam in. I can also remember Sunday brunches downtown on Fifth Avenue in the old Brevoort. He was a baseball fan and spoke of John J. McGraw and Christy Mathewson with awe. (Babe Ruth hadn't been heard of yet.)

There is one story about him I'd like to set down. As a schoolboy in Utica he worked afternoons for a Mr. Woolworth, who ran a little notions store where they sold buttons and needles and thread and shoestrings and anything else that cost ten cents or less. He did this for years for Mr. Woolworth, until he finished school. Then he heard of a job he could have in the Remington Typewriter Company down in New York City, and he told his friend and employer he was off.

Mr. Woolworth at that time was casting around for a little venture capital to open a few more five and tens, hoping for a little better profit margin. He did everything he could to keep my father with him, even offering a partnership. But Remington's appeal was stronger. "There's no future," my father said, "in this trivial nickel-and-dime stuff." Thus did he fail to be a part of the F. W. Woolworth Company, all because of the Remington Typewriter—and, I suspect, the lure of the Big Apple.

As a child I seem to have been average and happy. I specially loved baseball, either hard or soft, and played all infield positions. In summers I was a constant swimmer, belonged to the Boy Scouts, had a Swanson (noncapsizable) canoe on the Monongahela in West Virginia, loved "upriver camping" along the Tygart River Valley. In high school I loved acting and still remember how I enjoyed being Uncle Vanya in Chekhov's *The Cherry Orchard*. I imagine I was a standard American boy and read a magazine with that very title; I sold the *Saturday Evening Post* and set up sarsaparilla and birch beer stands when the circus came to town.

I liked most of my mother's family all right, though not all of them; they struck me as pretty dull: farm folk from Doddridge County. To tell the plain truth I had some hot exchanges with my mother about them, and more than once I told her defiantly, "I refuse to be tied down to a lot of boring and ignorant people I'm related to only by the sheer chance of birth." It grated on her sense of what's proper, I'm sure.

Her genealogy ran back, through many generations of William Davises, to the third son of the Lord High Sheriff of Cardiff; he came to the wilderness with William Penn's second expedition, toward the end of the seventeenth century. He was a Quaker in Philadelphia, after a career as an ex-Anglican preacher and Quaker in the Midland shires. The reverend colonist seemed to have a built-in tendency to the heretical and unorthodox. He first shocked the Friends' Meeting by arguing that they should all be baptized, and next he published a huge tome to prove that everybody should take Saturday rather than Sunday as the Lord's Day. That was too much; the Friends expelled him. As a result he founded the first indigenous Christian sect in America, the Seventh-Day Baptists.

My mother's own father, whom I barely remember, was William Francis Marion Davis, a sawyer; he fought in the

Confederate army, apparently for no special reason except that all the others on farms in Doddridge County and along the Ohio were fighting for the Union. As a girl my mother had been hooked into their peculiarities until she herself revolted— a revolt that took her up to New York in a dash for independence and a bigger world. In her nonfamilial moods she'd mutter sometimes about "those country jakes." Her "seventh day" childhood experience and her broken marriage, combined, kept her away from churches until she was in her late seventies; then she got caught up in a rather fundamentalist but nonchurch movement called the Missionary Alliance.

As a fatherless boy I showed my independence fairly early. My Uncle John in Buckhannon was like a father to me, but when he harped on the subject of what bastards the union miners were, something inside of me said he was off the track and I'd better not buy it just because he said so. I wanted to find out for myself.

I worked one summer of my high school years in the Consolidation Coal Company's office, as an assistant on the auditor's staff, posting books; and then the next summer—to my uncle's great disgust—I balanced things out by working as a trapper boy in a small unorganized coal mine operated by Mr. Reppard, a next-door neighbor of my other uncle, Will Morris, in Kingwood.

By hindsight I can see how immature and premature all of this was. I finished high school in only three years instead of the standard four, and then I did the same thing at the state university in Morgantown—which I entered at the age of sixteen. I was known in my fraternity there, Theta Chi, as the Infant. It was only about thirty miles from Fairmont, where my family lived, but even so it was as far away as my mother would let her still damp young son go.

My sympathies went out whole hog to the miners and to the cause of the United Mine Workers of America. That put me against the coal operators. And soon it set me more broadly against "the capitalist system." I still loved my Uncle John, of course, but I held solidly to my position even though I felt a little like Commodore Vanderbilt's mistress, Tennessee Claflin, who risked a break with him by publishing a weekly in which she expounded free love and socialism. (In one issue she exposed the famous preacher Henry Ward Beecher's love affair with the wife of a prominent journalist; it sold out at a black market price of forty dollars a copy.)

At this point I was still reading *American Mercury*, filling myself every month with Mencken's contempt for the "booboisie"—those who later, in the sixties, came to be called "squares" and "the establishment." It was some years after this before I graduated to *The New Masses* and a love affair with Marxism. Nevertheless, as early as my first year at the university I was already singing Joe Hill's Wobbly (IWW) songs.

The years after the First World War were a time when everything was radical: radical flappers, radical workers, radical writers. I nourished myself on Jack London, Lincoln Steffens, Mary Heaton Vorse, Floyd Dell, Louis Untermeyer, Anna Louise Strong, John Reed, Clarence Darrow's pleadings, and the five-and-ten-cent Little Blue Book pamphlets sold broadcast by Haldeman-Julius somewhere out in Kansas. It was a time of radical questioning. Eugene Debs polled nearly a million votes for President in 1920 while he sat in prison because he protested sedition proceedings under the Espionage Act. Along with many of my contemporaries, I was radicalized.

The term "radicalized" appeared during the students' revolt in the sixties, but it would have fitted many of us in the twenties too. Trying to reconstruct this radicalization in my own case implies all the risks of error that memory runs, plus the subjectivity of autobiography, but let me at least try to explain why or at least how it came about.

A math teacher in my high school named Claire Harkins introduced me to George Bernard Shaw's plays and their prefaces. They were what started me thinking; thinking, that is, critically. Nobody among my family or acquaintances had ever shown any intellectual interest. I was galvanized by Shaw, turned on. The Blue Books introduced me to history, philosophy, the concept of social justice, plays, poetry, and classical essays: for example, Charles Lamb on roast pig, Karl Marx's *Communist Manifesto*, and Clarence Darrow on the absurdities of the Bible. Mixed into Shaw's things and the Blue Books were a lot of explicit praises of socialism, with persuasive arguments for it.

Even though I was still a boy in high school I talked a lot about Mencken and Nathan. I was fascinated by what I found in their green-covered monthly, *American Mercury*. It contributed a great deal to my own radicalization; although the editors were too cautious mentally to expound or defend an ism of any kind, the steady stream of ridicule they poured on the dishonesties and pretensions of the status quo, both religious and secular, fed my growing scorn of the existing social order.

I was, of course, faced constantly with the question, "If you don't like what we've got, what are you going to put in its place?" Pondering about that, I convinced myself that the basis of social justice, or its absence, lies in the social structure that underlies all social relations and culture, and that what was needed was a new system—that social sanity was more than just a matter of values and attitudes. As a boy of fourteen and fifteen I found that new system in socialism.

Besides Claire Harkins I knew at most only a handful of others, all fellow high schoolers, who could and would talk about these things—who enjoyed and were not put off by my Shavian quips and sarcasms. By count I think there were only five. We formed a secret society and called it the OH Club, OH being the symbol in chemistry (so we were told) for a base radical.

Fairly early in my first year at the university I was jailed, but only overnight, for defying an injunction against speaking in public for the union. It was out at Scott's Run. By then I was carrying a union card (I applied for it) and had made enough impression somehow to be taken on part time on the workers' education staff of District Seventeen, UMWA. I was not, as I remember it, an obnoxious obsessive-compulsive radical. I was a socialist, yes, a left-winger whose sympathies were in the Mother Jones tradition, favoring Powers Hapgood and the rank-and-file movement, bucking the conservatism of John L. Lewis. In the

Socialist Party's internal struggles I backed Debs and the left rather than the Hillquit-Berger right. Still and all, I had a lot of time for and a hungry interest in philosophy and history, as well as fraternity life and bull sessions galore with all sorts and conditions of students.

Strong as my idealism was (social, never philosophical), I never became a pacifist. Most people at the university supposed I was one because it was known that I'd refused after the first year to take any more military training—required of all men students there by the terms of a land grant that went back to the Civil War. The point is that my reason for refusing was not a religious one.

What I said was that I would take no part in "fighting for the capitalist system." That tore it. The authorities shut the door on me, saying I'd never get a degree. They would, they conceded, let me stay and go on with my studies. Before me they'd had a few conscientious objectors, a minuscule few, who based their objection on religious grounds; they were excused from the military requirement. In my case, no. If you refused out of faith in a different world to come, one brought on by God's doing eschatologically, it was tolerated, but if you refused out of faith in a different kind of society to come by man's doing you were outside the pale.

The knowledge that I would not graduate brought me great freedom intellectually. I read widely, chose courses without regard to majors and minors, and spent my time thinking. It was philosophy mostly that gobbled me up. Thinking was what had got me in trouble in the first place, first in high school and now here at the university, so I simply went in for more and more of it. Students were expected to pass courses, I told myself, not to think. (To show how young I was at that time, I would always pronounce Socrates with a long *o*, on the ground that in Greek it was spelled with an omega, not an omicron.) If at that time anybody had said the university would confer an honorary doctor's degree upon me in 1984, an L.H.D., I'd have laughed till I fell down.

Two big things happened in my second year: I met my wife, and I got caught up in the church. The first was permanent. The second proved to be temporary—although it lasted forty years.

Forrest was named for General Nathan Bedford Forrest, the cavalry genius of the Confederacy, the one who in the oral tradition said that to win a battle you have to get there "fust with the mostest men." Her mother's father had played chess with the general at Sweet Chalybeate Springs season after season in the years following the war. Devoted to both of the Forrests, her grandfather always denied the "canard" that the general was the founder of the Ku Klux Klan, and also that he had any hand in the "massacre of Fort Pillow."

Forrest brought a complete and utterly final change in my life. I knew it instantly when I saw her for the first time, and although I tried to run away I failed because I just knew that without her I was and would be a complete nothing. It was more than sixty years ago when I first laid eyes on her, which is plenty of time to find out how right I was. The rest of that story is personal and private.

The second thing was ordination. Thus far I'd had no church experience. My mother was wholly nonchurch. My father had been a lapsed Catholic. But in Morgantown I got to know the rector of the Episcopal church, "Jocko" Horton. He was something new for me: brilliant, rational, sophisticated, and persuasive. (We saw him later in Honolulu just before he died—in his seventies.)

Out of many discussions at a weekly conversatz at his rectory, of the sort Voltaire liked to attend in Paris and Geneva, I formed two ideas. One was personal—that I could be admitted to theological school even without a bachelor's degree. The other was more grandiose; it was that in the church it was possible, with some hope of success, to bring social idealism to bear on church people and through them to give aid and comfort to the workers' struggle for economic democracy—not only in "industrial democracy" but at other levels throughout the whole social fabric. Christianity, I told myself, had a tremendous imperative for social justice, buried and lost sight of in the churches, and my job would be to get it out and working.

It was not Christianity that led me to my social ideals; on the contrary, my social ideals led me to Christianity. (The scenario is: Q. Why are you entering the ministry, young man? A. Because, sir, I want to do good in the world.) Here was a neat case of the pragmatic "will to believe," or what some of William James's students think he should have called "the decision to believe."

Off I went after three years of college to the Berkeley Divinity School, in Connecticut. This brief memoir is no place to explore the psychology of what I did. Lots of people have odd and bizarre reasons for professing belief in all sorts of things, secular as well as religious. The point is that my focus was passionately on Christian social thought and action, not Christianity as such. If instead I had looked at Christian ideas on their own merits, a good straight look, I'd have laughed the whole thing out of court.

At Berkeley I read hard and thought hard. I was lucky in finding a true comrade intellectually in my class there. He was Wilford O. ("Bill") Cross, son of a Methodist minister who had emigrated from England to Illinois. Bill first tried his vocation at the Holy Cross monastery, but they soon told him to leave and study for the ordained "secular" ministry. He too was immersed in philosophy, arguing constantly with me about pragmatism (which, as we shall see, was the most enduring part of my commitment) and constantly picking holes in socialism. Like me, Bill ended up as a professor of ethics and moral theology—in two seminaries, first a southern one and then one in the Midwest.

I find some irony now in remembering that one of the most rigorous intellectual experiences of those years was reading a book on Marxism by Max Eastman, an independently wealthy man who had financed the original (old) *Masses*. I read and underlined and margined and fine-picked that book until it was tattered and fell apart. I do not even remember now what its title was, but it utterly absorbed me. Eastman ultimately rejected the whole of the radical outlook. In the book I read at

Berkeley he was struggling against being what Eric Hoffer has since called a "true believer," and I suspect it was his struggle as well as his arguments that fascinated me. Starry-eyed simplistic Marxism never grabbed me, attracted though I was.

In the summer after our first year, Bill and I worked in a program called Seminarians in Industry. I was in the Plymouth Cordage Company factory in North Plymouth, Massachusetts, and Bill in a blanket mill in Fall River. I was soon taken off hemp and sisal sledges and made a cruiser in Mill No. 3, recording oil consumption in the rope-twisting machines. Rooting around in some files in my spare time on that job I found a blacklist, the existence of which the company men always denied. It was aimed at keeping union sympathizers out. I exposed them and caused something of a furor. Bart Vanzetti, the Italian anarchist, was heavily starred on the list. Some of what I learned there was used later by Upton Sinclair in his novel about the Sacco-Vanzetti case, *Boston*.

Out of that experience came my friendship with William Benjamin Spofford. Bill was both executive secretary of the Church League for Industrial Democracy (an Episcopal group) and editor of the church weekly *The Witness*. We shared the socialist idea pretty completely, although my theologizing about it usually left him cold. He'd print my pamphlets and articles, but he himself was an activist, a prodigious worker. We and our families were fast friends until his death in the seventies. Sharing a radical role in the church, we reinforced each other and endured the same condemnations. Our only serious split was over the Hitler-Stalin Pact on the eve of the Second World War, which he defended and I condemned.

In the second summer I worked as an unpaid errand boy for the historic Sacco-Vanzetti Defense Committee in Boston. I was hauled in by the police on the streets, the "Free Them" pamphlets in my pockets always incriminating me. Several times the police cordon at the State House picked me up, once on the same day that Edna St. Vincent Millay was arrested for inciting to riot because she wore a red raincoat. We spent the night together in the Charles Street jail.

The night I stood with thousands outside the prison while they executed their victims I swore solemnly to myself, as so many others were doing all across the world, never to believe anything "capitalist society" says and always see it as my enemy. Education, after all, is not a process; it consists of events too. Those were the days when A. Mitchell Palmer, as U. S. Attorney General, was giving us all a strong foretaste of what would come when Senator Joe McCarthy got under way in the early fifties.

The old pattern cropped up again. In the middle of my last year at Berkeley (the third), I was taken out on leave of absence to go to the national headquarters of the Episcopal Church in New York to collaborate with Spencer Miller (then deputy warden of New York's Sing Sing prison and education adviser to the AF of L). We were to investigate what became the title of a book, *The Church and Industry* (1930), which Miller and I published as co-authors. (Incidentally, I discovered I liked to write; poorly written as this first book was, it gave me a taste. I took a private vow not to write another one for twenty-five years, but I jumped the gun with *Christianity and Property* in 1947.)

I was chosen because of my earnest and somewhat oddball crusade for social action and economic democracy, even though still only a seminarian. Ordinarily, theological students were concerned with piety and church life, not social justice. One reason given by Dean Ladd for allowing me leave was that I was too young to be ordained anyway and would have to wait a year or more to reach canonical age. We were married in this period of leave. Forrest did research work for Margaret Sanger at her New York clinic, which at the time was still an illegal and criminal social service.

Thus began the Christian forty years of my life. I returned to Berkeley from New York to get my B.D. (now it's an M.Div.) and entered Yale Graduate School to study economic history. I also chaired New Haven meetings for Norman Thomas and other Socialist Party candidates—for example, Jasper McLevy, mayor of Bridgeport. Then I won the John Henry Watson Fellowship and in 1930 went to London to do further work under

R. H. Tawney, whose *Religion and the Rise of Capitalism* had been a great stimulus. For this I needed an A.B. I applied to West Virginia University, and on the strength of my theological identity they agreed to give it to me—if I'd come down and do a chemistry course in the summer. I did, and they did.

In London I divided my time three ways: at the London School of Economics, where I took a few lecture courses but mainly had sessions with Mr. Tawney; at the British Museum, digging into pamphlet material to learn what the seventeenth century's notion of economic morality was; and in a curacy at St. Peter's, Regent Square, preaching, saying and singing masses, running the men's snooker club, and taking the kids to the Lord Mayor's Guildhall beanos on Boxing Day.

By this time I'd altered my direction. At first the idea had been to be ordained and work somewhere—perhaps in Pittsburgh—in an industrial parish, giving active support to the workers in their struggle for a better society (which as a goal has long since been watered down in the unions' perspective). It was to be a practical ministry. However, after writing the book and investigating conditions and attitudes nationally in labor and church circles, it seemed to me that the first thing that had to be done was to excogitate and formulate the argument *theologically* for social justice.

I was not troubled too much about leaving practice to do theory. All through my life I've been in agreement with Marx's cognition principle, "the unity of theory and practice." I've always believed you have to do both to do either one well. The idea was not that you should practice what you preach—that is, be honest—it meant you should not preach if you don't practice, and vice versa. André Malraux's *Man's Fate*, his story of the Communist revolt in China, spoke of how he had to write "out of the vortex" of events to write well.

In short, theory divorced from practice is ivory tower stuff, and practice without theory is bumbling. In that spirit I did some speaking for Labour Party candidates, in by-elections in London and the Midlands. It was this lifelong principle of mine that led me later on to put so much emphasis on the case approach and the clinical setting, in medical ethics, and on actual situations when decisions and value choices are made.

This meant brainwork, of the sort that Harry Ward was already doing at Union and Reinhold Niebuhr was to do there later on, in a much less radical way. No Christian social action seemed possible until a more thorough job was done to explicate the "social gospel." First things have to come first, I decided, and this meant I must shift my energies to the scholarly and theoretical task. Even though my heart was in the front line my head forced me into the libraries and classrooms.

This is not the place to set forth the whole theology of social redemption that took shape in my thinking. Those who are interested can dig back into my books and published papers and pamphlets for the details. Let me say just this much. There were, I found, three rich resources to be run through my mental computer.

One was the social gospel of Walter Rauschenbusch and Washington Gladden and others of that genre. Professor Harry Ward was more or less in this stream. My complaint about their work was that, although ethically perceptive, it lacked adequate theological sophistication.

A second source was the League for the Kingdom of God, which published *Christendom*, "a journal of Christian sociology." I was a contributing editor for many years. This coterie of churchmen in England and the United States were theological enough but a bit too sectarian (Anglo-Catholic) to please me altogether.

The third important contribution to my thinking "Christianly" about social justice was by William Temple, Archbishop of York when I first knew him (and visited him) and later of Canterbury. To know how his social theology influenced me it is necessary to read my intellectual portrait of him, *William Temple* (1963)—written earlier but published within only a half dozen years of my auto-de-Christianization. (Of all my books, writing this one gave me the greatest pleasure.)

The core concepts of my social theology, when reduced to their essential terms, were along this line: that man is created essentially a social being, so individualism falsifies reality; that God created humankind for "membership one with another," giving social covenant a divine commission; that nationalism and racism and sexism are wrong (that is, false), and God's will is, through his church, to bring "fallen men" back into a radical solidarity; and that "redemption" means reordering society as well as changing individuals, the order or structure most authentically Christian being what in political language we might call democratic socialism.

This, of course, was expounded in often highly technical theological terms, and on grounds that socially conservative people were unable to tear down by theological reasoning; consequently they always had to resort to the well-worn objection, "It never has worked and therefore it never will." The conservatives in the churches held to the redemption of individuals only, not of society, as the true business of Christianity. But in those days I lived to the hilt by Paul's triad in First Corinthians 13: the theological virtues not only of love and faith but of *hope*.

The Great Depression brought us, Forrest and me, back to America. A teaching appointment I had at the Seabury-Western Theological School in Chicago's North Shore area was lost when my salary, as the dean there cabled, "went up the flue along with Sam Insull's utility bonds"—that is, they were wiped out in the current depression's fiscal crisis.

We came back because we felt we should be with our own people—share in their depression, unemployment, hunger, and fear. Before we came back I had three offers that might have kept us abroad. One was to be a vicar of St. Luke's Chapel, which was a student or campus ministry in the Cité Universitaire in Paris on the Left Bank. It was just not right for me. I was also offered an appointment teaching economic history at St. John's University in Agra, India, but I could see no strong reason to go. It was too far from the central action of the times. (Later we visited there, though, and also roamed the nearby Taj Mahal.)

The only hard one to turn down was the living at Painswick, near Stroud in Gloucestershire: a sinecure set up for people like me. It was a rectorial benefice, with its own independent income, needing no funds from Queen Anne's Bounty or the Ecclesiastical Commissioners. The terms of the living were that I'd only have to spend five weeks of the year in residence; all the rest of the time I could be away, as far away as Timbuktu if I chose, and all the visiting, preaching, marrying, and burying would be done by five curates! It was a famous plum, kept for the sake of scholars and thinkers. Ellis Roberts, literary editor of the *New Statesman and Athenaeum*, persuaded the bishop to offer it to me and we nearly took it. But not quite.

It's worth recording, by the way, that in another year the eminent William Inge, dean of St. Paul's Cathedral in London, retired and went to Painswick. My curacy at St. Peter's had been in the gift of the dean and chapter of St. Paul's, and I'd met Inge often enough to think of him as a deaf old curmudgeon. But getting the living at Painswick made him a mighty lucky one.

I had to buy groceries for my family when we got back to America, and after much frantic hunting I landed a job teaching in a junior college in North Carolina. It was St. Mary's in Raleigh, a distinguished school for southern young ladies, white: hardly my cup of tea, but I stuck it out for three years. In my third year, something happened that provides a kind of paradigm of my life in those days. It's worth telling, even at some length.

On the side I was teaching a course in labor relations at Chapel Hill, and a man named Ericson in the English department called me one day to say that he and Paul Green, the widely revered playwright, had been asked by a couple of striking textile workers to help them, as a matter of civil liberties. Would I come and talk it over? Yes. Over I went.

The nub of their story was that six members of the Piedmont Organizing Council of the United Textile Workers' Union, who had called the general strike then in progress, were now in jail, indicted for criminal conspiracy, namely, dynamiting the Burlington cotton mill. The company had two pieces of evidence: first, they said the men had actually carried out their dastardly plot, although they only succeeded in blowing up a little brick shed in the mill yard, with some old rusty machinery stored in it; second, two of the alleged members of the conspiracy had confessed.

It seemed absurd to us to think that months of planning to blow up the mill ended in a small explosion in a shed at a safe distance from the mill buildings and, furthermore, that the men who "confessed" to their guilt were well-known drunks, unable to get work in the mills because of their record and neither members of the union nor friends of any of the union members. It looked to us like a labor frame-up in classic form, of the kind quite common in those days. (By turning state's evidence, the two guttersnipes in the "conspiracy" would escape conviction and punishment, of course, and no doubt be well paid.)

Each of us undertook to see one of the accused in their jails. After insistent inquiry I was told that my man was over in Goldsboro in an infirmary prison. When I went there I could not see him, I was told; but I was wearing a clerical collar and when I threatened to return with a lawyer or court order the people at the jail relented and down I went to his cell. The turnkey stood just outside the door. When I got in and before I could say a word, the young fellow (he was the youngest member of the council) peered up at me and said, "I'll sign. I'll sign."

I could see his face was marked, his eyes red and sightless, and on the cot he moved his body with obvious pain.

I said, "You're not to sign anything. Hear me?" Then I explained why I was there and what we were going to do; we were going to get top-grade legal counsel in place of the two-bit local lawyers they had hired. We formed a Burlington Defense Committee and asked the national union to send us a big gun. The man they sent from New York was very able, but in the eyes of the public there, colored by the newspapers, he was a Yankee Jew Flannel Mouth. The county prosecutor won easily with a guilty verdict against the defendants, which meant against the union. Which meant for the company. We appealed.

The mill owner in Burlington was on the board of trustees of St. Mary's. One day I had a call from Bishop Penick. We lived next door to each other. He wanted to come over. In my study, in complete privacy, he offered me a choice: I could either resign from St. Mary's or resign from what he called, electrifyingly to me, the "Burlington Dynamite Defense Committee." He gave me two days to decide. It was a shock, for we were fast friends. I called Judge Connor, a justice on the state supreme court and also one of the trustees, and he let me come over first thing that evening. I told him the story.

When he heard me out he said, "I must be careful not to say or do anything *sub judice*. You have asked my advice. I think you should return to the bishop and tell him this: Judge Connor advises me that I have no problem of conflict between my role in the defense action and my work as a teacher at St. Mary's, but you think there is. Thus you have a problem, Fletcher does not, and you should make whatever decision you think is right, Bishop."

I told Penick this and it stymied him. He said he'd think it over. Since the ball seemed to be in his court, he waited for a meeting of the trustees' executive committee, of which he was chairman, the members including both the Burlington mill owner and Judge Connor. Meanwhile the Fletchers waited, wondering when we'd be out on the street—with our newborn son. I ran into Frank Graham one day (he was president of the University at Chapel Hill) and told him about it; he said, "Tell Ed Penick from me that any time he has no use for your services I need you at Chapel Hill"—a message I did not deliver.

Indeed, I never spoke again to the bishop. A friend, a young lawyer in Raleigh who was secretary of the trustees, told me that at the meeting Judge Connor walked up and down and orated about controversy, academic freedom, democracy, Christian concern for justice, the right to a full legal defense, a citizen's responsibility, the lawfulness of collective bargaining, and so on, until, in my friend's words, you could see the bishop getting "littler and littler."

Apparently the mill owner and the bishop were cowed by the supreme court justice. I received a formal letter from the trustees urging me to "limit my activities of a controversial nature"; that was all. I replied with a letter of resignation, to take effect at the term's end. And I acted out my reply by going down to Mt. Holly, near Charlotte, to conduct the funeral service for a striker who had been bayoneted to death by the National Guard as they moved in to break up a picket line; thousands of textile workers and their families were there. (This was at the request of an officer of the Federal Council of Churches, now the *National* Council.)

Fortunately, before the following Christmas I found work in Cincinnati. The bishop of Southern Ohio, Henry Hobson, told me that as a matter of episcopal courtesy he called Penick about me and Penick said, "Don't let Fletcher into your diocese. He's a troublemaker." In the nine years I was in his diocese Bishop Hobson often disagreed or disapproved of this or that I thought or did, but he was never "troubled" by it.

This has been a long account of just one incident but, as I said at the start, it is something of a type case or paradigm, in which all the elements of my life at that time are reflected. Incidentally, the upshot was that the Burlington case reached the North Carolina Supreme Court, where the trial court and other appellate rulings were all reversed and the union leaders exonerated.

Before the New Deal ended, the mills were organized. One of the men thus exonerated ran for Sheriff of Burlington County and was elected. Howard Mumford Jones had me come several times to his Harvard seminars to tell this story to his graduate students, in the fifties.

We had a summer and fall to wait before going to Cincinnati. We spent it at my mother's home, a charming little Vermont house in Grafton, near Bellows Falls. Always she was quick to come, whenever we needed her—for sick children, any crisis, any need: always steady, never cantankerous, giving herself quietly and completely and without exacting any quid pro quo. In her last years she lived with my sister, Mrs. Linus Emerson Kittredge, in Sands Point, Long Island, and died in 1961.

St. Paul's Cathedral in Cincinnati was in a common predicament. It was at first a rich people's place down in the fashionable

West End, but after a while those who could afford to moved out, up to the hills around the city, away from the heat and the Ohio River floods, and it became a slum for the most part. The remaining congregation could no longer pay for the cathedral's upkeep, and the diocese lost interest. Bishop Hobson asked me to be dean for a few years and then make a recommendation. My report said: Get rid of it, don't have a traditional cathedral.

We had a loyal but moneyless congregation, like St. Peter's in London. Once we had a WPA artist paint a reredos mural behind the Lady Chapel altar, modeled on Diego Rivera's famous fresco in New York's Rockefeller Center; it included faces of all races and peoples in the world in all walks of life, with Marx among them. Some of Cincinnati's noseybodies raised a fuss, demanding that it be painted out, but the bishop backed us against them.

The real reason for going to Cincinnati, where our daughter was born, was to build up a school of social training for seminarians that had been started ten years earlier by an ophthalmologist, William S. Keller. Dr. Keller had been convinced that the clergy needed to know more about community organization and its resources in casework and group work agencies, as well as medical services (hospitals) and correction programs (jails). In the early twenties he had started a summer vacation program of eight weeks. He had great creative imagination but he needed help; his free time was limited. Enlisting Bishop Hobson's support they cast around for a dean of what was now to be a full-time course, the Graduate School of Applied Religion. (Reinhold Niebuhr's chair at Union was in Applied Religion.) They fixed on me for it.

To make a long story short I added an eight-month session for junior clergy to the eight-week summer session for seminarians. I ran it for nine years. Altogether we turned out over five hundred people with certificates. The idea was to strike a balance between meeting individual human needs and training for social and community action too: a balance of the pastoral and prophetic sides of the ministry. Since then I have hardly gone anywhere in the United States where at least one of my "Cincinnati boys" was not active in local affairs.

After I gave up the cathedral, I also taught courses in labor history and New Testament (what a strange pair) at the University of Cincinnati, a splendid municipal university, and also social ethics intermittently in Hebrew Union College, for men entering the rabbinate of Reformed Judaism. I also taught and raised support for volunteer courses in a labor education night school supported by the local unions.

All through the thirties and forties and into the fifties I stuck to my socialist guns. This was the period when Communist Party theoreticians were transmuting Marxism into Leninism, at least to their own satisfaction; not to mine. They were in fact also replacing the proletariat with the Party—with a capital P, and I never could swallow it. They put non-Party people down as "mere" reformists, but I liked to claim some of us were true classical Marxists compared to some Party hacks. Backing the "united front" of Progressives, Socialists, and Communists was often a headache.

One of the things Claire Harkins gave me in my high school days was Bertrand Russell's *Roads to Freedom*, but I was so young I missed its warning. Russell explained that socialists "imagine that the Socialist State will be governed by men like those who now advocate it. This is, of course, a delusion. The rulers of the State then will bear as little resemblance to the present Socialists as the dignitaries of the Church after the time of Constantine bore to the Apostles."

Let me finish the passage: "The men who advocate an unpopular reform are exceptional in disinterestedness and zeal for the public good; but those who hold power after the reform has been carried out are likely to belong, in the main, to the ambitious executive type which has, in all ages, possessed itself of the government of nations. And this type has never shown itself tolerant of opposition or friendly to freedom."

Once I went down to Mississippi to teach labor history at an organizers' school of the Southern Tenant Farmers' Union, led by the radical preacher Claude Williams. They met on a farm near Clarksdale in the Delta, owned by the Rust brothers, who invented the first mechanical cotton picker. Twice I was beaten up by local rednecks and their sachems. They merged unionism, communism, and atheism into a satanic trinity. The thing they hated most was that we had blacks and whites in the same union and that we actually ate our meals together. Once I was caught by five men after dark near the farm and beaten with fists; the other time I was beaten unconscious with tire chains after they blocked my car at a lonely spot in the piney woods after dark. This was ten or fifteen years before the civil rights movement got started. (In that connection, I had Martin Luther King, Jr., as a student in several courses, while he was doing a Ph.D. in social ethics at Boston University's School of Theology in the forties.)

The result of my "united front" stance was that I was red-baited badly, especially in the McCarthy era, both from within and without the churches. It was, of course, only a part of my total life and work, but even a little bit of it was too much for the establishment. I was subpoenaed by Martin Dies of the House Special Committee on Un-American Activities (I called it the Un-American Committee) and by William Ezra Jenner of the Senate. At the same time, be it noted, the theological school did not dump me, as would almost certainly have been the case if I'd been teaching in a big secular university. Some of my colleagues, it is true, wanted me to resign, but the trustees, although antagonistic to my social goals, never fired me.

In England I had sought out the Christian Socialists, and in America for as long as he continued to run I voted steadily for Norman Thomas, a Presbyterian minister who succeeded Debs as the socialist leader. A lot of people voted Socialist, often just as a protest against the two status quo parties.

As to the "commies," I always held to the free market of ideas and urged people to go easy. "Don't outlaw them," I would say. "Outthink and outdo them." Christian Marxists, such as Conrad Noel in England and Francesco Nitti and his *Catholic Socialism* in Italy, were a rarity; in the forties and fifties they practically disappeared, only to crop up again here and there in the sixties.

Like most other radicals and many liberals too, I saw in events in Spain a kind of portent. When the Republic established in 1931 went from a left-wing socialist regime to a center-right one and then the pendulum swung again to a popular front government, only to be threatened finally by a fascist revolt with Franco's soldiers and Juan March's money, I fully supported the Loyalists.

The Spanish Civil War of 1936 to 1939 was, as I saw it, a struggle between reactionary fascist forces and democratic forces. When Roosevelt backed the Neutrality Act, which ended all U.S. sales to the Loyalists of military supplies, for the sake of the votes of Catholics (their church backed the Franco nationalists all the way), I wrote bitter editorials in *The Living Church*, a weekly on which I was an associate editor. I kept saying that the Neutrality Act was giving a green light to international fascism, and a general putsch in Europe would result.

Events proved I was right, although Franco left it to Hitler and Mussolini to do the job. The editor of *The Living Church*, a man named Morehouse, kicked me off for my "foolish" and "radical" views. And the U.S. Attorney General's list of subversive persons had Forrest and me on it as (it seems incredible) "premature antifascists"—that is, guilty of opposing fascism before it was officially recognized for what it was and before war was declared on it after Pearl Harbor in 1941.

Radicals, by the way, all opposed Roosevelt's New Deal; they looked upon it as "mere" gradualism and reformism. I began to discover in myself an increasingly conscious preference for a nondoctrinaire and nonideological social strategy. Although there was something I respected in those who made grandiose commitments to isms, I began to think I did not really believe that doctrinaire "solutions" would solve problems.

Now I can see more clearly than I did then that at a deep level I had a noncreedal bent eating away at me—eating away at my Christian ideology, by the way, just as much as it more consciously ate away at my socialism.

Perhaps the way to describe this nearly subliminal change going on in me would be to express it philosophically. At bottom I was still convinced by the case for pragmatism, in both the cognitive and ethical senses, which I had long since accepted as a convinced pupil of James and Dewey. The trouble was that a part of me responded to the strong appeal, we might even say the theater, of the "change agents" who worked often quite selflessly for socialism and found a rationale for their goals and methods in Marxism.

The termitic action, if I may coin a phrase, of my pragmatism brought me first to doubt the labor theory of value and Marxian economics as a whole, then to start qualifying the materialist interpretation of history, and finally to see that the whole doctrinaire thing was contradictory to pragmatism. (Later, the same contradiction was to crystallize around doctrinaire Christianity.) The fact is, of course, that pragmatists simply cannot be "true believers" in any grandiose ideology.

I remember flying from Cincinnati to New York, I think it was in 1942, to speak at a "second front" meeting in Madison Square Garden. Paul Robeson sang out of his barrel of a miraculous body ten feet away and the air thrummed. As I faced out on the twelve thousand people who packed the Garden I both thrilled to the scene and yet thought to myself, A war against fascism is a war against dictatorship, whether of the left or right—whether of the proletariat or the racists.

Again in 1950, in Prague, at a meeting of the World Peace Council, I felt in my bones, in the very atmosphere around me, that the society east of the Iron Curtain was deadly to personal liberty and there was no good reason to think differently or to hope for anything else from it.

At the same time I reasoned that the problem of peace in the world was the problem of how Communists and non-Communists could live together in the same world. I felt therefore that the World Peace Council deserved active participation because it was trying to bring the two together in meetings at the people's level, the unofficial nongovernmental level. Let Communists and non-Communists confront each other, I said—a policy that has since been adopted, of course, in many forms, in such things as mutual tourism, the Pugwash meetings, student exchange, official cultural exchanges, open-door conferences.

In the McCarthy ambience this brought instant punishment. For instance, the State Department would always deny passports to non-Communists wanting to attend Council meetings, or at least get other countries en route to deny them entrance visas, while at the same time they saw to it that known Communists got their passports and visas promptly—with the consequence that the meetings were dominated by Communists and could then be discredited as "Communist dominated." By this stratagem I was actually refused a British visa to attend a World Peace Council meeting in London.

As I write this in 1983 the same old struggle continues; it's still the number-one question of social ethics. The U.S.–Soviet face-off and the threat of nuclear omnicide is now in a far more exigent stage; it takes the shape of Armageddon. The nuclear-freeze initiative of American and Soviet scientists, physicians, and social activists in the early eighties is being described by President Reagan as either a plot by subversives in sheep's clothing or a movement of naive dupes led by the nose by Communists.

The same thing was said in the seventies about those who criticized America's role in Vietnam. My never having been a pacifist has given me no reason to be a war lover. I opposed the wars in Vietnam and before that Korea; in my time I've found my "just war" ethic has provided a sufficient reason for only the two World Wars—especially for the second one, the one against fascism and racial holocaust.

My experience tells me that sadly the old adage is true: thinking stops at the water's edge. When it comes to foreign affairs there is no way but what "we" are doing. Faced with external forces even a democracy turns tribal.

My last fling as a genuine leftist was to go to Australia in 1950 to a South-East Asia Peace Congress in Melbourne. It was fiercely red-baited. For several weeks afterward I barnstormed over Australia with the "Red Dean" of Canterbury, Hewlett Johnson. We spoke about how to make peace at the rank-and-file level, letting the diplomatic game take its own course. We got no support except from the left-wing unions and some of the clergy.

Here's an incidental story. I had long known Harry Bridges, famous leader of the longshoremen's union on the West Coast, and in a human gesture I called on his mother, who lived in the outskirts of Melbourne. She was a hard-bitten Catholic and told me, "I don't want to hear anything about him or from him. Go away."

To the constant question, "How can you talk seriously with Communists?" my reply was, "We have to; that is the heart of the problem of peace." My core concept was peaceful coexistence, and in those days even to use the phrase branded you in the eyes of many people as a crypto-Communist or at least a "fellow traveler."

I recall that when my plane reached the marine airport at Sydney I was dog-tired but found a bevy of reporters waiting to interview me. The newspapers were working overnight to discredit the Peace Congress. Their spokesman said, "Professor, are you aware that Communists are mixed up in this meeting you're going to?" I replied I'd had no information yet about the meeting's constituency. Then he said, "Well, it's true, and now that you know, what are you going to do about it?"

My answer was, "I'm travel weary and maybe I'm not doing your question justice, but I think that if what you say is true I ought to congratulate the organizing committee. The problem of peace is how Communists and non-Communists can live together in one world. Obviously they should be got together to talk about it together." That, of course, was not what he wanted.

From then on I was excoriated. In Melbourne the majority of the clergy boycotted the meeting, but they were uneasy about it and asked me to come to a closed-door session at Cathedral House with a couple of hundred of them, to explain my conception of peacemaking and its theology. They reenacted essentially the Sydney press corps confrontation all over again, only this time in clerical collars.

Socially sensitized people in those days were getting messages from every direction, and they weren't easy to sort out. In my own case my foundation convictions were limited in number, but I had some: three. One was that a better and more rational world, a sane society, is possible. Another was that the democratic principle is vital to all economic and political structures. Third, I was certain that to love justice means we have to balance somehow the two values—personal freedom and social covenant. These convictions were on the positive side.

At the same time I developed the perception that definition in negative terms as well as positive is necessary; that to say what something is *not* is what gives it real definition because it thereby becomes exclusive. I could see what communism was doing in Russia, and its Party activities were an offense to all my positive convictions—all of them. That was easy to see. But then I began to wonder if the democratic socialism I wanted was workable. Underneath my intellectual enthusiasms and rationalizations was that growing undercurrent of pragmatism.

The Communists had shown us by this time that if you ignore civil liberties in order to get socialism, the socialism you get cannot be democratic; and what I wanted most of all, I was able to see, was personal freedom and political democracy—even, if need be, at the expense of economic democracy.

This reversed what any "good Marxist" would say, of course. I still held to the desirability of the socialist ideal, but I was increasingly skeptical as to its workability. Perhaps I had been more shaped by Bertrand Russell's *Roads to Freedom* than I knew when I first read it in high school.

One hot summer day in Ralph Barton Perry's apartment, overlooking the Charles River, we had a long discussion. As a moral philosopher and a great one, he contended that there are two roads to social democracy. It can be reached either by setting up political democracy first and then extending it to the economic system, as in the Western world, or the reverse sequence could be followed as they were doing in Soviet Russia. I found I was rejecting Professor Perry's "reverse sequence." The English revolution, I felt, was not an accident of democracy; political democracy was essential, could not be secondary.

We might say I was beginning to feel about it as most people in Europe and America did. I too began to see that there is no viable alternative to a gradually changing capitalist social order. I threw myself more vigorously than ever before, therefore, into the construction of a reformist Christian social theology. For this reason the New Left rose and fell in the sixties with only marginal attention from me.

This could be seen in my new interest in business ethics, my teaching in the Harvard Business School's summer program for people who came from far and wide and my teaching of the Musser Seminar in business ethics in the winter terms. People would often say, "What! You're giving a course at the B-School? I don't believe it." It was during the summer session that I met Father Tom Wassmer, a Jesuit, then teaching moral philosophy in St. Peter's College, Jersey City, and soon I arranged to have him come as a visiting scholar to the Episcopal seminary: we ran seminars together in which the students claimed to develop "tennis neck" as we taught from opposite ends of the seminar table. Out of it came our joint book on situation ethics, *Hello Lovers!* (1970).

On the other hand, my lifelong commitment to civil liberties easily drew me over to civil rights, although after the march at Selma, Alabama, I was too caught up in the situation ethics thesis and in medical ethics to be an activist anymore. One of my students, Jonathan Daniels, was shot down in cold blood in plain sight of a segregationist mob (the man who killed the seminarian was found not guilty), and the bitter reaction to this plain injustice showed me that fair play had more appeal to the general run of people than socialism ever had or ever will.

All through this period, the forties and the fifties, I had been working hard at Christian theology and ethics. In actual fact I'd put vastly more time in on that task than on the social action I have described here. It was my work and my paid vocation to be "doing" Christian social ethics. And I delivered, all right. Bibliographies, periodicals, and the news stories of the period record it. The American Society for Christian Ethics got its start with Jim Adams of the Harvard Divinity School as its president, and I succeeded him in an election held at the Yale Divinity School in New Haven in the early sixties.

My rejection of the doctrinaire and the dogmatic bore its fruit in my best-seller, *Situation Ethics*, to my great and welcome surprise. The publisher heard me read a paper at the Alumni Visitation Day at the Harvard Divinity School in May 1965, and asked me to write a little book, for "intelligent laymen as well as clergymen." I started work on it on June 29, and on August 4 I sent them the completed typescript. In truth it was only an outline of situation ethics (I've always called it "my fat pamphlet"), yet it met with a tremendous response. Its thesis was set forward within the context of Christian rhetoric, but situation ethics as a theory of moral action is, of course, utterly independent of Christian presuppositions or beliefs. (I like knowing that I've contributed to the English language: Webster's now lists "situation ethics" and gives an excellent pithy definition.)

My main principle, that concern for human beings should come before moral rules, and that particular cases and situations are more determinant of what we ought to do than "universal" norms are, was applauded in the helping professions (medicine, social work, public administration, clinical psychology, and so on) but generally condemned by Christians, Jews, and Muslims—most of all by the orthodox ones.

After all, with an absolute God, his word revealed and his will eternal, how could relativity in ethics get anywhere with them? I find it significant, however, that the book was attacked just as fiercely in Marxian journals, such as *Trud* in Moscow and *Science and Society* in America.

My earlier book *Morals and Medicine*, the Lowell Lectures of 1949, had shown that my concern with social ethics was not a monomania. I had developed the biological focus too. My book was recognized to be the first of its kind, a modern non-Catholic treatise on medical ethics; it too made some history, here in America and in translation in Africa, Asia, and the Middle East. It is generally said nowadays to be the pioneering work of a new discipline, biomedical ethics—a new discipline that quickly won an important place for itself in the sixties and seventies.

Morals and Medicine led, when I retired from the Episcopal Theological School, to my being made the first professor of medical ethics in the School of Medicine at the University of Virginia.

Retrospectively, I see a four-phase history of ethics in my time. Back in the twenties when I got started in ethics we turned to the social sciences for data and insights: to economics, political science, cultural anthropology. Concern with social ethics, as distinguished from interpersonal, was not yet widely accepted, especially not in the curricula of either secular or theological schools. Then in the thirties there was a discernible shift of focus in ethics, this time to the behavioral sciences, especially psychology, from which we hoped for and got some help with basic notions such as "will" and "determinism" and "value choice."

In the forties and fifties we made a third shift, to the physical sciences, due chiefly perhaps to two things, nuclear power and various ecological imbalances. Most of us, however, had been trained in the humanities and were unable to cope with right-wrong judgments when they depended on technology based on physics and chemistry. Even so we could see their impact on human beings and values, and out of that phase emerged a new sensitivity about nuclear energy, weaponry, and protection of the environment.

(I learned a lot quite directly about the moral philosopher's helplessness when I sat on the medical technology panel of the Congressional Office of Technology Assessment for a few years in Washington. It was humiliating but also exciting and stimulating.)

Beginning in the seventies there came yet another, a fourth, shift of attention in ethics—this time to the biological or life sciences. Its leading edge was medical ethics, which broadened to biomedical ethics, which then became "bioethics." It was inevitable that I should be part of it. I was in great demand at the outset as a lecturer and writer in the field, not only because of *Morals and Medicine* but also because of *Situation Ethics*, my more recent theoretical book.

It's of interest that the first people to do serious work in the field of medical ethics were religiously oriented moralists. By April 23, 1980, I had spoken in 415 universities, colleges, medical schools, and seminaries. In addition, I was a speaker, visiting fellow, or guest in forty-five schools abroad, in Europe, Asia, and Australia. Philosophical ethics continued to be tied up in semantic analysis or metaphysics, and professional philosophers only came into bioethics slowly, as Johnny-come-latelies.

My own ethics, as I tackled value problems and the right-wrong issues posed by medicine and biological innovations, was essentially humanist—humanist in the sense of nontheist. Like Protagoras I saw man as the measure of things, the determiner of value and truth, not God or a revelation of any kind.

On the other hand I have never been a humanist in the sense of one who idealizes human beings. Like Mark Twain, I see on the record that it can't be done. In any event, by 1970 I had settled firmly for the consequentialist position that the right thing to do in any case is whatever will maximize human benefit, regardless of supposedly relevant but abstract moral rules.

This situational way of looking at value problems, which leaves aside all grandiose and "ultimate" theories of good and evil, took full hold of me at a meeting on social justice held in Geneva by the World Council of Churches. Bishop Brooke Mosley, once my student in Cincinnati, asked me to go. I found their way of looking at social issues in terms of prefabricated doctrines of Christian theology was by now alien and irritating. I could not help but compare it to the humility and exact knowledge I always found in Geneva at the World Health Organization when I'd attend their medical ethics sessions.

My nondoctrinaire approach to problems not only ran me straight athwart religious social ethics but also religious personal ethics too—for example, the notion that abortion is wrong as such because it violates "God's will." It set me over against those who condemn test-tube reproduction or the termination of badly defective newborns at birth, on the ground that these things, to use their language, are "against nature."

In two summary words, I was at last a *humanist situationist*—in matters both personal and social. It used to bug me, by the way, when occasionally I'd read that some of my old comrades-in-arms in social ethics had accused me of abandoning the problems of social justice because, they said, my focus now was on the biological rather than the political or economic front— as if they were separable.

Why this totally new career, at—of all things—the ripe old age of sixty-five? I'm sure part of the answer lies in the fact that I had de-Christianized myself. Three years before I was due to retire from the Episcopal school I faced it at last and finally— faced, that is, the final realization that social justice was not going to get any significant help from Christian social ethics, and the churches were never going to plow any new and important ground.

It was a bitter draught. It forced me to take a hard look at Christian doctrine itself, on its own merits: God, Jesus, revelation, sin, salvation—the whole repertory. Looking at it like that, I said to myself what I no doubt often glimpsed along the way, that the whole thing was weird and untenable. And along with Christianity went all ideology of any kind. I had reached what is expressed in the title of a book by Daniel Bell, *The End of Ideology*.

So this was the end product of all my thinking up to 1967, as it had been recorded in a half dozen books, sixteen chapters written for symposia, fifty-four articles, and twenty-one pamphlets and monographs. I may have been wish-thinking all that time, but I wasn't being lazy. Nor was I lazy in the fifteen years of active work that followed. By 1984 I more than doubled the amount I had published prior to 1967.

Pascal said it's not necessary to hope in order to undertake, nor to succeed in order to persevere. This may be true psychologically for some people, but for me it's not and never has been. When I embraced socialism and Christianity I simply *had* to believe they would work, and when that hope died I had to forsake them. I had to pull loose when history and my own personal experience finally convinced me they were precious as ideals, rationally indefensible, and inconsequential.

William James explained why the will to believe withers when nothing is won by believing. I backed off and said, swallowing hard, "What an absurd story, that God created the world, let men be as wicked and weak as they chose, then waited until only two thousand years ago before he picked out an obscure peasant in Palestine to redeem the world, decreeing that the only way human beings can escape the eternal damnation he himself imposes on them is to believe that the Palestinian is by a divine power their savior, which fixes everything up just right for the believers—but not for his fellow creatures."

I told my colleagues and students at the Episcopal Theological School (this was, remember, in 1967) that I could no longer take part in chapel services. I was, I said, still a theologian in the sense that I had a special knowledge of theology, but now I was an alienated or unbelieving theologian. I still am, of course, and always will be.

As I said later, in a kind of *apologia pro vita sua* written for an editor who requested it, when I de-Christianized I went through no "dark night of the soul" such as John of the Cross detailed. Instead, it had been an experience of freedom and comfort, of mental calm—although sometimes with a slight ambivalent sense of loss. For forty years I lived in the church. I left it to keep faith with myself, but without anger and with lots of thanks to it for many things.

Going to the medical school at the University of Virginia in Charlottesville to teach biomedical ethics was a perfect way to begin my new life. And without any doubt whatsoever the most telling part of it all was Dr. Thomas Harrison Hunter. He and I had met earlier, and right at the start we clicked. When I arrived he had just stepped down from the deanship, and as Owen Cheatham Professor of Science in the university he was free to join me in a humanities enterprise. We set it up as the Program in Human Biology and Society, to deal with the ethics as well as the social context of medicine.

Tom was my teacher as well as my friend and colleague; he helped me to "biologize" my thinking knowledgeably, joined me in innumerable analytic discussions, kept his door open to me constantly (we shared offices and seminar room), and never once—as far as I could see—did he ever fail to disagree with me when he saw reason to.

We might say that Tom medicalized me, but it was Garrett Hardin, social biologist at the University of California at Santa Barbara, my rare good friend Garrett, who biologized me. Garrett and I were first comrades in the struggle to legalize abortions.

There were some in the field of medical ethics who looked askance at my participation in activist groups such as the Society for the Right to Die, a voluntary euthanasia league of which I was president for a while, and the Human Betterment Society, now the Association for Voluntary Sterilization, of which I was also president one term. We have made great progress on all these fronts. It's hard for young people, I imagine, to realize that in my time these things were not only morally condemned but legally criminal.

As I used to tell people, nobody would believe how much I learned after I was sixty-five years old. It went a long way beyond what I used to know and do in the ethics seminar for Harvard med students in their clinical years, meeting once a week in the old Bullfinch Tower at the Massachusetts General Hospital. Back in those days, in the fifties and sixties, medical ethics was still little more than an avocation with me, but the Virginia School of Medicine made it a full-blown vocation: my new life.

When I reached the age of seventy-two I had to yield up my visiting professorship because of a university statute limiting the age for that rank, but they kept me on by creating something called Visiting Scholar for me. Of the books I published after I started teaching at Charlottesville, I think the one that makes manifest my new outlook was *The Ethics of Genetic Control* (1974), but some say *Humanhood: Essays in Biomedical Ethics* (1979) is a more revealing mirror of my thinking and teaching.

As I was given the Beecher Award in 1981 for my "pioneering role in biomedical ethics," and again in 1982 when the national council of Alpha Omega Alpha, the honors medical society, elected me an honorary fellow (the only humanist on their roll of non-physicians, the others all being scientists), I felt like saying, The thing you've honored me for is built on the ashes of two other things that burned out on me: Christianity and socialism. My work in biomedical ethics is something like a phoenix, the beautiful bird that arises from the ashes of a funeral pyre.

Something heartwarming happened in 1983, the year I actually and effectively retired by requesting an end to my appointment at the University of Virginia. I was told that my writings on situation ethics had made it possible to settle an internal policy issue among the Iroquois or Six Nations, who thereupon took me into the Mohawk or Canienga Tribe, Clan of the Turtle—with the name Ro-he-hon (forceful teacher). A letter about it came from Tehanetonens, in the Moon of the Sweetwater (March), ending with: "May our Elder Brother, Sun, shine strong in your lodge."

Prior to going to the University of Virginia, I—and often Forrest too—had traveled a lot: coast to coast, Central America and Mexico, India and North Africa, the Caribbean (all the islands except Jamaica), both sides of the Iron Curtain in Europe, but only one side of the Bamboo Curtain in Asia. But after the explosive takeoff of biomedical ethics in the seventies, I spent a good third of my time airborne on lecture engagements, especially to medical schools and medical meetings.

Another heartwarming thing was Richard Taglar's dedicating his new volume of philosophy to me in 1984, *Reason, Faith and Ethics*. His teaching and writing at the University of Rochester had long had my admiration. I'd begun to think I would shuffle off this mortal coil with no book dedicated to me, until he wrote me what he'd done. His note came happily just as I read that we both, he and I, were given our places among the laureates of the Academy of Humanism, along with such luminaries as Stephen Jay Gould, Carl Sagan, Sir Karl Popper, Francis Crick, Isaac Asimov, Edward O. Wilson, Sir Alfred J. Ayer, W. V. Quinn, Lady Barbara Wootton, et al.

I have to confess also that a new motivation lay behind this sometimes exhausting work: money. We faced old age with no resources but a church pension and social security benefits until the royalties on *Situation Ethics* started coming in. The lecture fees paid me in my new life were considerable, and to be quite candid I flew everywhere as much for the pay as for the cause. It was a new factor in my outlook and a new way of thinking ahead. What I earned I turned over to Forrest for investment and her good management. Had it not been for this we might have become a burden on our children, or at least a concern for them.

Don't think of me as a harassed or embattled person. I was not; not at any point. In Freudian terms I've always had plenty of ego strength. Not that I was ever overbearing or strident. On the contrary, people who hated or challenged my ideas always liked me personally (and I them). This, I suppose, was because I've always related easily to others, of all stripes, and I related easily, I suppose, because I liked people—as people.

My ego not being brittle or weak, I could always move along in the face of difficulties and opposition. I was never kept out of things because my positions were unpopular, as I might have been if I'd been the sorehead type or loaded with hostility. On the contrary, my life has been one of much comradeship and belongingness and acceptance as a person, for which I'm thankful. All my life I've found that we can stretch each other's tolerances a very long way if we keep hatred out—as distinguished from indignation.

I remember being greeted by the economist Kenneth Boulding, a visiting professor at International Christian University just outside in Tokyo at the same time I was, 1963—1964: "Well, well, I'm glad at last to shake the hand of the infamous Red Churchman"—humorous and accepting, but still a little skittish. We have run into the same kind of thing many times, in Europe, Latin America, even in Thailand and the Philippines.

In the spring of 1964, believe it or not, the U.S. State Department, via the embassy in Tokyo (my son Joe's colleague at Harvard, Edwin Reischauer, was ambassador at the time) sent me up to the University of Hokkaido to lecture to the economics faculty on William Temple's World War II proposals for a new economic order, which I had fairly fully outlined in my book, *William Temple*. So now, at last, State was using me instead of trying to squelch me.

What all this comes down to, in summary fashion, is that I went through two intellectual phases in my adult life. The first was as an ideologue and doctrinaire, which took shape in two guises, Socialist and Christian. The first to die out was the socialism, then the Christianity. My second phase has been as a relativist, empirical, and far humbler intellectually—humbler about what I suppose to be true and about what I suppose I can know.

Radicals, as I see in retrospect, are the people who speak up too soon. I remind you that Forrest and I were once listed by the Department of Justice as "premature antifascists." Radicals are the ones who first protest, liberals are the ones who join them when their protest has begun to be heard, and conservatives accept or at least live with what the liberals finally win. This is worth some meditation. Still in retrospect, and with no attempt at an exhaustive account, let me mention some things that I and my fellow radicals got started toward ultimate acceptance by our society, however grudgingly and slowly: I'll put them down in two categories, hardly more than by title.

In matters of social ethics and social justice we have seen the abolition of yellow-dog contracts, which once made not joining a union a condition of employment; the abolition of the injunctive power of courts to take away personal freedom; the abolition of Jim Crow unions and hiring practices; the end of segregation in schools and public places. The right to organize and bargain collectively has been established; the right to vote and other civil rights are solidly in law; the right to travel has been forced on the bureaucracy, ending the practice of refusing passports on political grounds; the transcript of the Sacco-Vanzetti trial is used as a lesson in what not to do in the courts; the right to know has legally opened the records of so-called congressional inquiries; and equal rights for women have been accepted, although far short of fully, and even though ERA has not been adopted.

In matters of biomedical ethics I have seen legal and medical triumphs for such "radical" innovative practices as artificial insemination and inovulation, in vitro fertilization (test tube babies), genetic engineering, brain-death statutes, germ and embryo freezing, the patient's right to know, transsexualization, and DNA splitting and recombination. We have won the wars for voluntary abortion and sterilization and will soon have completed the roster of states with right-to-die laws. All these things and more, in both categories, were radical by definition and by general sentiment, and yet all of them have been won. Let it not be said that radicals are ineffective—only that they tend to pay a lot personally for what they gain, as liberals do not—at least comparatively.

Nor are those who read this to suppose that I had a hard, frustrating, embittering life. It was good, all of it. I knew many people, of all kinds and stations, in many parts of the world; had an exciting intellectual life, a superb family; lived in pleasant homes almost always, some of them beautiful; and our children had the great advantage of top-grade schooling and friends.

I worked hard, for long hours. Yet with long fallow periods too; academic summer vacation and sabbatical leaves are a blessing. I have always believed in the work ethic; not in the sense that those who don't work should not eat, but in the sense that those who do not work, as distinguished from a mere job to survive, live unsatisfactory and unfulfilled lives.

My life seemed to come full circle in a meaningful way when the president of West Virginia University called me in the early spring of 1984 to say I should come to Commencement to receive the honorary degree of Doctor of Humanities, on nomination by the School of Medicine there. At once I could see in my mind's eye the earnest and eager boy of sixteen who arrived there as an undergraduate in 1922.

This memoir might come as something of a surprise to some. Most people today know little or nothing of the radicalization of my early life. They might have heard or read of my de-Christianization, and some might call that radical, or if their ethics consists of the old morality based on rules rather than situational variables they might think of my work in moral philosophy as radical. But they no longer know me a *social* radical.

Incidentally, the longer I live the more persuaded I am that the word "radical" should never be used as a synonym for "extreme." Properly, it can only mean "going to the roots" of a question or problem, which is exactly what the word means literally and originally.

This is very much a no-frills accounting of my life. After all, it is not an autobiography and was never intended to have the rich detail that any personal history worthy of the name would have. At most it is a sweeping story, aimed at providing my family—for whom it was written at their request—with a more or less chronological record of the essentials only. Nothing more.

Forrest and I have seen fit to write out a hundred or more anecdotes or vignettes, arranged in a very loose time order with the idea that each one stands on its own bottom, and they should go a long way toward filling in the story in this memoir with more circumstantial and more human remembrances. Like salt and pepper, they can be used according to taste. I am even inclined to think that the anecdotes may yield a more truthful picture than this pro forma memoir. Writing about yourself is a lot trickier than writing about what you've seen or done.

Works by Joseph Fletcher

BOOKS

1930 *The Church and Industry* (with Spencer Miller). New York: Longmans, Green & Co.

1947 *Christianity and Property* (ed.). Philadelphia: Westminster Press.

1954 *Morals and Medicine: The Moral Problems of the Patient's Right to Know the Truth.* Princeton, N.J.: Princeton University Press.

1963 *William Temple: Twentieth-Century Christian.* New York: Seabury Press.

1966 *Situation Ethics: The New Morality.* Philadelphia: Westminster Press.

1967 *Moral Responsibility: Situation Ethics at Work.* Philadelphia: Westminster Press.

1970 *Hello Lovers! An Introduction to Situation Ethics* (with Thomas Wassmer). Ed. by William E. May. New York: Corpus Books.

1974 *The Ethics of Genetic Control: Ending Reproductive Roulette.* Garden City, N.Y.: Doubleday & Co., Anchor Press Book.

1979   *Humanhood: Essays in Biomedical Ethics*. Buffalo, N.Y.:
        Prometheus Books.
1988   *The Ethics of Genetic Control: Ending Reproductive
        Roulette*. With a new introdcution. Buffalo, N.Y.:
        Prometheus Books.

CONTRIBUTIONS

1960   *Contemporary Theology*, ed. by T. K. Thompson. New
        York: Association Press, 204–227.
1965   "William Temple." *Handbook of Christian Theologians*.
        Ed. by Dean Peerman and Martin Marty. New York:
        World Publishing Company, 233–255.
1966   "Anglican Theology and the Ethics of Natural Law."
        Christian Social Ethics in a Changing World. Ed. by John
        C. Bennett. New York: Association Press, 310–329.

        "Die Ethik des Naturrechts." *Die Kirche als Faktor einer
        kommenden Weltgemeinschaft*. Ed. by W. A. Visser 't
        Hooft. Stuttgart-Berlin: Kreuz, 162–179.

        "Love and Justice Are the Same Thing." *Lux in Lumine:
        Essays to Honor Norman Pittenger*. Ed. by R. A. Nor-
        ris. New York: Seabury Press, 129–143.

        "Opinion Is Divided." *Abortion and the Law*. Ed. by David
        Low. New York: Simon & Schuster Pocket Books.
1967   "Ethics and Unmarried Sex: Morals Reexamined." *The
        99th Hour*. Ed. by D. O. Price. Chapel Hill, N.C.:
        University of North Carolina Press, 97–112.

        "The Protestant Churches." *Birth Control: A Continuing
        Controversy*. Ed. by E. T. Tyler. Springfield, Ill.:
        Charles C Thomas, 99–196.

        "Situation Ethics Under Fire." *Storm Over Ethics*. Ed. by
        the publishers. Philadelphia: United Church Press,
        149–173.
1968   "About the Case Study Method." *The Ethics of Decision
        Making*. Ed. by Malcolm W. Eckel. New York: More-
        house-Gorham, 13–19.

"American Pragmatism and the Problem of Theological Ethics." *Religion in Modern Society*. Ed. by W. H. Baumer. Buffalo Studies V. Buffalo: State University of New York at Buffalo Press, 90–110.

"Elective Death." *Ethical Issues in Medicine: The Role of the Physician in Today's Society*. Ed. by E. Fuller Torrey. Boston: Little, Brown & Co., 139–157.

"Medicine's Scientific Developments and Ethical Problems." *Dialogue in Medicine and Theology*. Ed. by Dale White. Nashville: Abingdon Press, 101–133.

"What's in a Rule? A Situationist View." *Norm and Context in Christian Ethics*. Ed. by Gene H. Outka and Paul Ramsey. New York: Charles Scribner's Sons, 275–301.

1969   "A Minister's View." *Therapeutic Abortion*. Ed. by J. F. Hulka. Chapel Hill, N.C.: Population Center, 37–39.

"Our Shameful Waste of Human Tissue." *The Religious Situation 1969*. Ed. by D. A. Cutler. Boston: Beacon Press, 223–252.

"The Patient's Right to Die." *Euthanasia and the Right to Death*. Ed. by A. B. Downing. London: Peter Owen, 61–70.

"A Theological Approach to Prolonging Life." *But Not to Lose*. Ed. by A. H. Kutscher. New York: Frederick Fell, 115–117.

1970   "Love Is the Only Measure." *Situationalism and the New Morality*. Ed. by R. L. Cunningham. New York: Appleton-Century-Crofts, 55–64.

1975   "A New Look Inside." *You're All Right, Jack* (honoring John Oliver Nelson). Kirkridge, Pa.: Kirkridge Center, 3–4.

"The Right to Live and to Die." *Beneficent Euthanasia*. Ed. by M. Kohl. Buffalo: Prometheus Books, 44–53.

1976   "Computers and Distributive Justice." *Ethics and Health Policy*. Ed. by R. M. Veatch and Roy Branson. Philadelphia: J. B. Lippincott Co., 197–215.

"Ethical Considerations in Biomedical Research Involving Human Beings." *Proceedings, International Conference on the Individual and the Community*. Ed. by Bruce Dull. Geneva: World Health Organization/World Medical Society, 121–142.

"Ethics and Feeding the Starving." *Lifeboat Ethics: Morality and Hunger*. Ed. by George Lucas. New York: Harper & Row, 53–72.

"In Verteidigung des Suizids" (trans. Günter Seib). *Suizid und Euthanasie als Human- und Sozial-wissenschaftliches*. Ed. by Albin Eser. Stuttgart: Ferdinand Enke Verlag, 233–244.

"No, Not to My Family You Don't." *Proceedings, Medical Social Consultants, National Conference of Social Welfare*. Ed. by R. White, 61–64.

1977   "Give If It Helps But Not If It Hurts." *World Hunger and Moral Obligation: Philosophical Perspectives*. Ed. by H. LaFollette and W. Aiken. Englewood Cliffs, N.J.: Prentice-Hall, 77–99.

"Situation Ethics." *Encyclopedia of Bioethics*. Ed. by W. T. Reich. New York: Free Press-Macmillan Co.

ARTICLES

1931   "Catholic Social Reform in the Third Republic." *Stockholm* 3, 255–277.

"The Spirit of Capitalism: Weber's Work." *Christendom: A Journal of Christian Sociology* (Oxford) 1 (Mar.), 55–62.

1933   "Religion in Social History: Ernst Troeltsch." *Christendom: A Journal of Christian Sociology* (Oxford) 3 (Sept.), 207–210.

1934   "A Case Study in Moral Theology." *American Church Monthly* 35 (Jan.), 38–43.

"The Church and Social Credit." *Spirit of Missions* 99 (Apr.), 173–176.

"Religion and Capitalism in History." *Christendom: A Journal of Christian Sociology* (Oxford) 4 (June), 138–142.

"Was the Early Church Communistic?" *Living Church* 91 (Nov. 17), 615–617.

1937 "The Condition of Our Times." *Anglican Theological Review* 19 (Apr.), 119–131.

1939 "The Catholic Family: A Sociological Approach." *Christendom: A Journal of Christian Sociology* (Oxford) 9 (Mar.), 26–35.

1960 "Modern Prophets: Novels." *Episcopalian* 125 (Dec.), 30–33.

1962 "Dythanasia." *Folia Medica* 8 (Jan.-Mar.), 3–8.

"Anti-Dynasthia: The Problem of Prolonging Death." *Euthanasia Society Bulletin* 15 (Spring), 1–8.

"The Professions: A Theological Frontier." *Episcopal Theological School Bulletin* 54 (July), 6–12.

1963 "The End of the Era of Common Sense." *Religion in Life* 32 (Spring), 238–246.

"A Moral Tension and an Ethical Frontier." *Christian Scholar* 46 (Fall), 256–266.

"Changing Sexual Mores: Towards a New Judeo-Christian Consensus," *Current* 44 (Dec.), 6–14.

1964 "Christian Ethics in a New Key." *Annals* (International Christian University, Tokyo), 165–197.

"Death and Medical Initiative." *Prism: The New Christian* (London) 92 (Dec.), 18–24.

"Doing the Truth: James Pike's Social Ethics." *Church Review* 22 (Dec.), 10–12.

1965 "About Edmond Cahn." *New York University Law Review* 40 (Apr.), 215–216.

"Family Dysfunction, East and West." *Pastoral Psychology* 16 (Apr.), 34–38.

"Sex and Situation Ethics." *Living Church* 151 (Nov. 21), 10–11.

1966 "The New Morality: Ethics at the Crossroads" (with Herbert McCabe, O.P.). *Commonweal* 83 (Jan. 14), 427–440.

"The Changing Church: What Is the New Morality?" (with Herbert McCabe, O.P.). *Current* 71 (Mar.), 59–64.

"Why New? The New Morality." *Religion in Life* 35 (Spring), 187–190.

"The New Morality: A Debate." *Extra* (University of Houston) 3 (June), 8–9.

"Christianity, Not Religion," *Pulpit* 37 (July-Aug.), 18–21.

1967 "Christian Ethics in a New Key: Commentary." *Perspective* (Kenyon College) 3 (Winter), 3–7, 19–21.

"The Issue of Culpability." *Sandoz Psychiatric Spector* 4 (Nov.), 8–9.

1968 "Situation Ethics, the New Morality." *Alumni Magazine* (Rockford College), 45 (Winter) 12–17, 27.

"Tillich and Ethics: The Negation of Law." *Pastoral Psychology* 19 (Feb.), 33–40.

"Rats and Ghettoes." *Episcopal Theological School Bulletin* 60 (Mar.), 16–17.

1973 "Medicine and Criteria of Human Nature." *Science, Medicine and Man* (Oxford) 1 (Sept.), 93–102.

"The Control of Death." *Intellectual Digest* 4 (Oct.), 82–83.

1974 "New Definitions of Death: The Richmond Brain Case." *Prism* 2 (Jan.), 13–14, 16.

"Medicine, Morals, and Religion." *Theology Today* 31 (Apr.), 39–46.

"To Live and Die." *Humanist* 34 (July-Aug.), 12–16.

"Abortion and the True Believer." *Christian Century* 91 (Nov. 27), 1126–1127.

"Four Indicators of Humanhood: The Enquiry Matures." *Hastings Center Report* 4 (Dec.), 4–7.

1975 "Situation Ethics and Watergate." *Theology Today* 31 (Jan.), 343–345.

"Being Happy Being Human." *Humanist* 35 (Jan.-Feb.), 13–15.

"Situation Ethics, Law, and Watergate." *Cumberland Law Review* 6 (Spring), 35–60.

"Dead or Alive: A Definition." *Cross Talk* 4 (June), n. p.

"Fetal Research: Pragmatists and Doctrinaires." *Hastings Center Report* 5 (June), 11–46.

"On the Hartford Declaration." *Theology Today* 32 (July), 185–186.

"Who Has First Claim on Health Funds?" *Hastings Center Report* 5 (Aug.), 13–15.

"William Howard Melish: 40th Anniversary of His Ordination." *Churchman* 189 (Aug.-Sept.), 12–13.

1976 "Feeding the Hungry: An Ethical Appraisal." *Soundings* 59 (Spring), 52–69.

1978 "Ethics and Recombinant DNA Research." *Southern California Law Review* 1:6 (Sept.), 1131–1157.

1979 "The Cerebrum: Key to Truly Human Life," *Science, Medicine and Man: An International Journal* 1:3 (Fall), 21–23.

1983 "Secular Humanism: It's the Adjective That Counts." *Free Inquiry* 3:4 (Fall), 17–18.

1985 "Residual Religion," *Free Inquiry* 6:1 (Winter), 18–19.

"Ethics, Politics, and Human Reproduction" (with T. H. Hunter). *Pharos*, Alpha Omega Alpha Honors Medical Society, Menlo Park, Calif. 18:4 (Fall), 55.

1986 "Ethics Ponder Bioengineering." *Daily Progress*, Charlottesville, Va., May 4, F3.

"Ethics for the 21st Century." *Religious Humanism* 24 (Spring), 8.

"Geriatric Psychiatry: The Case of the MI, DNR, ECT, NG, and DOD." *Psychiatric Annals* 16:7 (July), 411–413.

"Guns and Suicide: A Personal Opinion." *Hemlock Quarterly* 24 (July), 8.

"Diminishing Returns." *Free Inquiry* 6:4 (Fall), 53–54.

1987 "The Courts and Euthanasia." *Law, Medicine, and Health Care* 15:4 (Winter).

"The Moral Dimension in Clinical Decision Making." *Pharos*, Alpha Omega Alpha Honors Medical Society, Menlo Park, Calif. 50:2 (Spring), 2–4.

"Medical Resistance to the Right to Die." *Journal of the American Geriatric Society* 35:7 (July), 676–682.

"Education and Free Inquiry." *Free Inquiry* 5:3 (Summer), 4.

"A Secular Humanist Confesses." *Free Inquiry* 7:3 (Summer), 36.

"Humanism and Theism in Biomedical Ethics." *Perspectives in Biology and Medicine* 31:1 (Fall), 106–116.

"Euthanasia in the Courts." *Euthanasia Review* 2:3 (Fall), 15–22.

1988 "Humanism and Theism: A Conflict?" *Witness* 71:2 (Feb.), 12–15.

"Ethics and Old Age." *Update* 4:9 (June), 3–6.

"On Truth-Telling." *Pharos*, Alpha Omega Alpha Honors Medical Society, Menlo Park, Calif. 51:2 (Spring).

MONOGRAPHS

1928 *The Church and Industrial Relations: A Preliminary Report.* New York: National Council of the Episcopal Church, 31 pp.

1933 *What Is Christian Sociology?* Problem Paper Series (No. 1). West Park, N.Y.: Order of the Holy Cross, 32 pp.

1934 *Bibliography on the Church and Industry* (with Spencer Miller). New York: National Council of the Episcopal Church, 17 pp.

The Church and Social Credit. Facing 1934 Series (No. 4). Ed. by C. Rankin Barnes. New York: National Council of the Episcopal Church, 8 pp.

Money Makers and Moral Man. New Tracts for New Times (No. 9). New York: Morehouse Publishing Co., 14 pp.

1935 *Christian Doctrine and Social Action.* New York: Church League for Industrial Democracy, 18 pp.

1939 *The Church and Its Community.* Church in Urban America Series (No. 4). New York: National Council of the Episcopal Church, 23 pp.

1941 *The Meaning of the Malvern Declaration.* New York: Church League for Industrial Democracy, 11 pp.

ANTHOLOGIES

1966 "The Patient's Right to Die." *College Reading and Writing*. Ed. by W. Johnson and T. M. Davis. Chicago: Scott, Foresman, & Co., 420–428.

1967 "Euthanasia: Our Right to Die." Ed. by I. W. Knobloch. New York: Appleton-Century-Crofts, 425–426.

"The Fletcher-McCabe Debate." *Contemporary Religious Experience*. Ed. by E. B. Fiske. New York: Bobbs-Merrill Co., 28–40.

"Medical Ethics." *A Dictionary of Christian Ethics*. Ed. by John Macquarrie. Philadelphia: Westminster Press, 210–212.

"The Patient's Right to Die." *The Enquiry Reader*. Ed. by E. I. Sullivan et al. Boston: D. C. Heath & Co., 95–103.

1968 "Three Approaches to Social Morality." *Contemporary Religious Issues*. Ed. by D. E. Hartsock. Belmont, Calif.: Wadsworth Publishing Co., 247–255.

Various Readings. *Dimensions of Decision*. Ed. by N. J. Wert. Nashville: Methodist Publishing House, nos. 80, 86, 98, 113, 119, 122.

1969 "Our Shameful Waste of Human Tissues." *Updating Life and Death*. Ed. by D. A. Cutler. Boston: Beacon Press, 1–30.

1971 "Ethics and Unmarried Sex." *Moral Issues and Christian Response*. Ed. by P. T. Jersild and D. A. Johnson. New York: Holt, Rinehart & Winston, 108–117.

"Love Is the Only Measure." *The Language of Argument*. Ed. by D. MacDonald. Toronto: Chandler Publishing Co., 68–79.

"The Patient's Right to Die." *Success in College*. Ed. by M. H. and E. S. Norman. New York: Holt, Rinehart & Winston, 102–109.

1972 "Ethics in Logics and Values." *Right and Reason*. Ed. by A. J. Fagothy, S.J. St. Louis: C. V. Mosby Co., 111–124.

"Morals and Unmarried Sex." *Perspectives on Human Sexuality*. Ed. by J. L. Malfetti and E. M. Eidlitz. New York: Holt, Rinehart & Winston, 71–79.

"Six Propositions." *Ethics in Perspective and Practice*. Ed. by W. K. Sites and B. C. Blossom. New York: Oceana Publications, 41–44.

"Voluntary Euthanasia, the New Shape of Death." *Experimentation with Human Beings*. Ed. by J. Katz. New York: Russell Sage Foundation, 716–717.

1973   "The Relativity of Moral Judgment." *Introduction to Philosophy*. Ed. by P. E. Davis. New York: Charles E. Merrill Publishing Co., 66–75.

1974   "The Case of Euthanasia." *Problems of Death*. Ed. by David L. Bender. St. Paul, Minn.: Greenhaven Press, 63–70.

1975   "Euthanasia: Our Right to Die." *Ethical Issues*. Ed. by W. R. Durland and W. H. Bruening. Palo Alto, Calif.: Mayfield Publishing Co., 220–247.

1976   "Ethics and Genetic Control." *Bioethics*. Ed. by T. A. Shannon. Boston: Paulist Press, 319–326.

"Ethics and Health Care Delivery: Computers and Distributive Justice." *Ethics and Health Policy*. Ed. by R. M. Veatch and R. Branson. Cambridge, Mass.: Ballinger Publishing Co., 99–109.

"Indicators of Humanhood." *Bioethics*. Ed. by T. A. Shannon. Boston: Paulist Press, 319–326.

1977   "Ethical Aspects of Genetic Control: Designed Genetic Changes in Man." *Ethics in Medicine*. Ed. by S. J. Reiser et al. Cambridge, Mass.: MIT Press, 387–393.

1978   "Designed Genetic Changes in Man." *Matters of Life and Death*. Ed. by J. Thomas. Toronto: Samuel Stevens, 144–153.

"The Ethics of Genetic Control." *Contemporary Issues in Bioethics*. Ed. by T. L. Beauchamp and L. Walters. Belmont, Calif.: Dickson Publishing Co., 585–587.

"The Medical Revolution and Religion." *Readings in Religion: From Inside and Outside*. Ed. by R. S. Ellwood, Jr. Englewood Cliffs, N.J.: Prentice-Hall, 319–321.

"Pediatric Euthanasia: The Ethics of Selective Treatment of Spina Bifida." *Decision Making and the Defective Newborn*. Ed. by C. A. Swinyard. Springfield, Ill.: Charles C Thomas, Publisher, 477–488.

"The Right to Know the Truth." *Ethical Issues in Death and Dying*. Ed. by T. Beauchamp and S. Perlin. Englewood Cliffs, N.J.: Prentice-Hall, 146–156.

1979 "Death and Decision." *Euthanasia: A Decade of Change*. New York: Concern for Dying: An Educational Council, 48–55.

"The Ethical Implications of Genetic Control." *Prospects of Man: Genetic Engineering*. Ed. by J. G. Little. Toronto: York University Press, 103–116.

1980 "Humanistic Ethics: The Groundwork." *Humanistic Ethics*. Ed. by M. B. Storer. Buffalo, N.Y.: Prometheus Books, 253–261.

"Situation Ethics." *Constructing a Life Philosophy*. Ed. by D. L. Bender. St. Paul: Greenhaven Press, 67–73.

1981 "Cost and Benefits, Rights and Regulations, and Screening." *Biomedical Ethics*. Ed. by T. A. Mappes and J. S. Zembaty. New York: McGraw-Hill Book Co., 475–478.

"In Defense of Suicide." *Suicide and Euthanasia: The Rights of Personhood*. Ed. by S. L. Wallace and A. Esser. Memphis: Tennessee University Press, 38–50.

From *A Reader in Theological Ethics*, ed. by T. J. Beale. Pretoria: University of South Africa Press. "Love Is the Only Norm," 38–47; "Abortion," 50–58; "Our Duty to the Unborn," 72–101; "Humanness," 193–201; "Infanticide," 237–247; "Suicide," 254–264; "Euthanasia," 310–320; "Cerebration," 342–349; "Wasting Human Bodies," 351–367.

1983 "Ethical Aspects of Genetic Control." *Ethical Issues in Modern Science*, 2nd ed. Ed. by J. Arras and R. Hunt. Palo Alto, Calif.: Mayfield Publishing Co., 401–407.

1985 "Euthanasia." *Textbook of Christian Ethics*. Ed. by Robin Gill. Edinburgh: T. & T. Clark, 480–483.

"The Impact of Unbelief on Moral Judgments." *The Encyclopedia of Unbelief*. Ed. by G. Stein. Buffalo: Prometheus Books, 459–467.

"Justice." *Powers That Make Us Human: The Foundation of Medical Ethics*. Ed. by K. Vaux. Champaign, Ill.: University of Illinois Press, 93–104.

"Situation Ethics." *Textbook of Christian Ethics*. Ed. by Robin Gill. Edinburgh: T. & T. Clark, 135–143.

1986 "Hippocratic Oath." *Westminster Dictionary of Christian Ethics*. Ed. by J. F. Childress and J. Macquarrie. Philadelphia: Westminster Press, 149–150.

1987 "The Ethics in Genetic Control: Some Answers." *On Moral Medicine*. Ed. by S. E. Lammers and A. Verhey. Grand Rapids: Wm. B. Eerdmans Publishing Co., 348–362.

"Foreword." *The Home Front*. Ed. by Vera Kopelman. New York: Vantage Press, vii.

"Four Indicators of Humanness: The Enquiry Matures." *On Moral Medicine*. Ed. by S. E. Lammers and A. Verhey. Grand Rapids: Wm. B. Eerdmans Publishing Co., 275–288.

"Technological Devices in Medical Care." *On Moral Medicine*. Ed. by S. E. Lammers and A. Verhey. Grand Rapids: Wm. B. Eerdmans Publishing Co., 220–227.

1988 "Ethics and Genetic Control." *Medical Ethics: A Guide for Health Professionals*. Ed. by J. E. Monagle and D. C. Thomasma. Rockville, Md.: Aspen Pubs., 3–11.

"Naturalism, Situationism, and Value Theory." *Ethics at the Crossroads*. Ed. by G. F. McLean. Washington, D.C.: Catholic University of America, n. p.